## Praise for *Seven Steps to Confident Writing*

"The blank page can strike terror in the heart of any would-be writer. Alan Gelb has the remedy: simple, practical steps that turn a daunting task into a process anyone can master."
— **June Casagrande**, author of *The Joy of Syntax* and *It Was the Best of Sentences, It Was the Worst of Sentences*

"Alan Gelb offers practical direction and inspiring models to guide even the reluctant writer forward. In his book *Seven Steps to Confident Writing*, Gelb shows readers how to engage in the writing process and how to embrace the elements of style that will lead to writing success whether you are writing an office memo or a movie script. 'Writing requires enormous effort,' writes Gelb, but as a master coach he guides readers toward the 'enormous satisfaction in bringing a piece of writing to its best state.' This is an important book that I look forward to sharing with my students and others who need practical writing guidance."
— **Sandra Marinella**, author of *The Story You Need to Tell*

"As a writer and teacher of writing, I find *Seven Steps to Confident Writing* by Alan Gelb to be exceptionally helpful. I have Gelb's quotes on index cards propped around my work space. His advice is succinct and clear. Reading Alan Gelb's book charges me with renewed energy, and I find myself heading for my latest draft to polish and refine the work."
— **Tina Welling**, author of *Writing Wild*

D0052060

"In *Seven Steps to Confident Writing*, Alan Gelb proves that confident writing is a skill that can be taught. He lays out practical steps and clear guidance that any writer can follow to edit and strengthen his or her writing. I look forward to using this resource with my own writing students."
— **Denise Jaden,** author of *Fast Fiction* and *Story Sparks*

"Alan Gelb demystifies good writing in a tone that's both warm and no-nonsense. What shines through is his own love of writing — the fundamentals, the precision of language, the structure of sentences (including my favorite sentence from *Stuart Little*), the search for your true voice, and the lapidary work of rewriting. He modestly asserts that if you're looking to write a novel or memoir, this may not be the book for you, but I disagree. This is a book for anyone who wants to be a better writer — no matter what your experience."
— **Barbara Abercrombie,** author of
*A Year of Writing Dangerously*

"At the same time that writing skills are deteriorating, people in all walks of life — solo entrepreneurs, managers, engineers, and millions more — are obliged to communicate well. Writing is the skill needed today, and Alan Gelb's *Seven Steps to Confident Writing* is an essential guide for anyone who must write in order to stay competitive."
— **Eric Maisel,** author of *A Writer's Paris*

# SEVEN
# STEPS
# TO
# CONFIDENT
# WRITING

## Also by Alan Gelb

*Conquering the College Admissions Essay in 10 Steps:*
*Crafting a Winning Personal Statement*

*Having the Last Say:*
*Capturing Your Legacy in One Small Story*

# SEVEN STEPS TO CONFIDENT WRITING

## ALAN GELB

New World Library
Novato, California

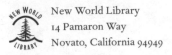 New World Library
14 Pamaron Way
Novato, California 94949

Text design by Tona Pearce Myers

Library of Congress Cataloging-in-Publication Data

Names: Gelb, Alan, author.
Title: Seven steps to confident writing / Alan Gelb.
Description: Novato, California : New World Library, [2019] | Includes
     bibliographical references and index.
Identifiers: LCCN 2018047668 (print) | LCCN 2018060995 (ebook) |
     ISBN 9781608685455 (e-book) | ISBN 9781608685448 (print : alk. paper) |
     ISBN 9781608685455 (Ebook)
Subjects: LCSH: Authorship--Handbooks, manuals, etc.
Classification: LCC PN147 (ebook) | LCC PN147 .G43 2019 (print) | DDC
     808.02--dc23
LC record available at https://lccn.loc.gov/2018047668

First printing, March 2019
ISBN 978-1-60868-544-8
Ebook ISBN 978-1-60868-545-5

Printed in Canada on 100% postconsumer-waste recycled paper

 New World Library is proud to be a Gold Certified Environmentally
Responsible Publisher. Publisher certification awarded by Green Press
Initiative.

10   9   8   7   6   5   4   3   2   1

# Contents

Introduction                                                        ix

Step One: **See the Big Picture**                                   1

Step Two: **Gear Up**                                               31

Step Three: **Tell Stories**                                        63

Step Four: **Revel in the Amazing, Expandable,
     Elastic, Evolving Sentence**                                   93

Step Five: **Move from Draft to Draft**                             129

Step Six: **Watch Your Tone**                                       161

Step Seven: **Do the Lapidary Work**                                199


Acknowledgments                                                     241

Index                                                               243

About the Author                                                    255

# Introduction

We hear much in the media about the death of the written word and how woefully deficient today's students are in writing skills. Although there may be solid empirical evidence to back up such claims, I work year in and year out with high school students, and I don't see such a dire problem. The majority of my students possess basic writing competencies, even if they don't seem to value or enjoy the act of writing very much. For the most part, they know how to string sentences together and have some understanding of paragraph structure, but they don't seem to have ever experienced the pleasure that comes with hitting that writing "sweet spot."

Within a week or two of our working together, however, I often see significant improvement in both attitude and accomplishment. My writers begin to understand that writing is not something you get right or wrong, but rather is something you work at — arduously, exactingly, even achingly, but sometimes with delight. They come to see that writing lends itself to collaboration in which writer and editor both play a part, and they commit themselves to the work, which can be fun and ultimately rewarding.

In the relatively brief time that we intersect, these writers, at first indifferent to the work, start to make a case for why a certain word or phrase should be preserved, even if I suggest otherwise. As we labor in the trenches together, they assert their sense of ownership over their work and demand to be honored as writers. And, of course, I accord them that honor, thrilled to see their investment in their product.

Interestingly, among the legion of students I have coached, only about two or three stand out in my mind as having been exceptional writers whose prose possessed the kind of energy and flow that really cannot be taught. Those individuals had a love of language, a confidence in their articulation, and the ability to order their thoughts — all qualities that placed them well ahead of their peers.

On the other end of the spectrum, I can still recall a few students whose writing was distinctly below par. Even the simplest of sentences could trip up these folks, who sought to disguise their tenuous grasp of sentence structure by applying all kinds of gewgaws to their writing, from inappropriate adjectives, to unnecessary adverbs, to misconceived metaphors, and of course my pet peeve: exclamation points! Those students — really, just a handful out of so many — made me hang my head in despair, at least for a while, not sure what I could do to help.

Head hanging aside, however, I have come to realize

how much my writers have benefited from the short writing tutorial that we go through together. They learn about such things as:

- Writing to an audience
- Forming a "contract" with their reader
- Clarity and brevity
- Writing as a process
- Understanding the structure of a sentence
- Approaching an assignment
- Sensitivity to tone
- The power of vocabulary

Even if my students have had some passing familiarity with these matters, I have found that the concentrated nature of our time together allows valuable lessons to sink in.

In 2015, I published a book called *Having the Last Say: Capturing Your Legacy in One Small Story*. This book encourages people of a certain age — let's call them baby boomers — to engage in an act of life review. They write a 500- to 1,000-word narrative that focuses on an ethical value they have lived by, with the idea of leaving this work as a keepsake for their loved ones or a reading for their own memorial service. Interestingly, working with this older population of writers has shown itself to be not all that different from the work I do with my high-school writers. So far, none of my adult writers have been truly exceptional, and none have been significantly below par. Their basic writing skills are decent, but their writing does not come alive until they start to understand more about the overall writing process. I have even worked with a few professional writers on these short life-review pieces, and, as a result of this work, they too have gained new insights into the craft of writing.

What is quite fascinating to me is that these writers often show marked improvement in just a matter of a week or two. This is what led me to the idea of a seven-step program that could promise development in as little time as I am describing. In fact, I think it is entirely possible for a person's writing to show positive changes in just a short amount of time — and, these days, many of us can only devote a short amount of time to the various things we take on. That's just a fact of modern life. Although we may no longer be carrying coal or wringing out laundry, so many of us still manage to be time-poor.

Now let me caution you. If you are looking to write a terrific novel, play, or screenplay, this is not the book for you. If you are looking to write a full-fledged memoir, this is probably not the right book either. If you are looking for strategies to make your academic writing fly, here too you will need to do supplemental reading. If, however, you have never felt settled into the act of writing and it has always been somehow alien to you, then this book may change your life. I know what "alien" feels like. I missed some weeks of school back in the day when long division was being taught, and somehow I've never gotten divisors and quotients quite right. Calculators handily take care of my long-division deficit, but unfortunately nothing so simple exists to help those who feel uncomfortable or even clueless about writing.

In fact, writing is a basic form of human expression that should feel natural and not be accompanied by great pain. Speaking of pain, I have endured several bouts of sciatica at various points in my life, and during one such siege I learned some movements from a good friend who is a Feldenkrais therapist. The Feldenkrais Method, named for the distinguished scientist Moshé Feldenkrais, is based on the premise that many of us, as we grow older, simply forget how to move naturally. Feldenkrais devised simple movements and small exercises that are designed to help people rediscover the efficient and graceful movements that our bodies are engineered to carry out and that somehow get undone by our acquired habits. In essence, the Feldenkrais Method teaches people to relearn their intuitive movements.

During this dose of Feldenkrais therapy, I found myself on the floor, executing little crawling and reaching movements like those I did a *very* long time ago when I was a baby, and I was astonished by the benefits I felt right away. I have been reminded of that experience many times when working with writers who seem to have gotten off on the wrong foot with regard to their writing. Their writing agony reminds me of my lower-back problems, and the very simple "movements" I teach them quickly ease their pain.

Anyway, here you are, holding this little book in your hands. Perhaps you have already bought other books on writing, and nothing has worked for you. You're still hoping that something may come along to deliver you from your feelings of insecurity and inadequacy. You want to become a better writer, and so you should. After all, writing is vitally important.

If, for instance, you are seeking a refund after a horrible motel stay, you will need to be able to write a letter of complaint. If you wish to make a toast at your daughter's wedding or say parting words at the funeral of a dear friend, you will need to gather your thoughts and put them into words. If you are deeply disturbed by the idea of hydrofracking in your area, you will want to write to your member of Congress or your local newspaper. If you are applying to a program in massage therapy or mechanical engineering, you must be able to order your thoughts in writing so you can make a case for yourself.

If you want to reclaim writing — a basic strength that you have somehow been deprived of — then now is the time. This book will take you kindly, gently, and firmly toward your goal, as I help you become a better writer in just seven steps.

## STEP ONE

## See the Big Picture

One reason so many people experience fear when they sit down to write is because they have not yet thought about who it is they are writing to or for. A letter to Grandma and a letter to the editor should not sound the same (unless Grandma happens to be the editor). Identifying the reader is a valuable action that can help people get over the first of many writing humps.

When you understand that you are writing *for* someone, you feel less alone with a piece of writing — even if the person who eventually reads what you have written is somehow intimidating, as with a teacher, a critic, or a potential employer. It is helpful in any case to realize that an actual person will be on the other end of this communication and that the job is either to inform, amuse, or persuade that person (or do all three concurrently).

So when I am writing to a customer-service representative

at a motel chain about a shoddy experience I have had, I want to start out by visualizing that person. In reality, she may be someone who gets a lot of complaints but who tries to be truly responsive to them all. On the other hand, she may be someone who doesn't particularly value her work or pay much attention to what comes her way; she simply signs a form letter and encloses a coupon for a free breakfast the next time you happen to stay at the Last Resort.

Now, keep in mind that you won't know who that person is when you write your letter of complaint and you won't know how she functions in the world, but you can certainly create an *ideal* person — someone who is responsive, who listens, and who will act on your complaint. Creating such a prototype will inspire you to write more effectively rather than just spout and fume, which rarely does much good.

Whenever I discuss the issue of communication with writers, I can see how important and clarifying it is for them to visualize their reader. For instance, when my high-school students set out to write their college-admission essays, I ask them to imagine themselves sitting at a party next to somebody they do not know.

"How do you want that person to think of you as a communicator?" I ask them. "Do you think it wise to spout your achievements and try to impress that person with what you have accomplished? Or is it better to make a real interpersonal connection with that individual, so that he or she will be open to finding out more about you as you continue to communicate?"

The latter is always the right answer.

You can fall short on the communication front in a

number of distinct ways — and it's altogether possible that your communication style could be afflicted by several of these shortcomings at the same time. Consider the following:

- **The insecure communicator** is the mumbler who evades your eye as he swallows his words. He has little conviction in what he has to say, so he says it as quietly as possible, often trailing off so that he won't even be noticed.
- **The inconsiderate communicator** does not keep her listener's needs in mind. She interrupts, does not pick up on cues, and can be strident.
- **The inappropriate communicator** intrudes on the space that most people try to maintain in social intercourse. He talks too close to you, reveals too much about himself, and does not know when to stop talking.
- **The inaccessible communicator** is aloof and comes across as cold. She doesn't connect with her listener, because she doesn't feel the need to make connections.
- **The inexact communicator** says one thing and means another. He gets tripped up in his own discourse, and because he cannot be counted on to keep up his end of the conversation, an exchange with him often goes nowhere.

Communication can go awry between two people in other ways, but these cover quite a few problem areas — and the interesting thing is that these problems apply to written language just as much as to spoken language.

Recently, I worked with an autistic college applicant who was mainstreamed in his high school and did very well academically. He decided to write something about the stigmatizing condition with which he had been struggling all his life. I certainly agreed that something so central to his identity should be brought into his college application, and the personal statement seemed a good place to explore this subject. We worked together on an essay about his pet lizard, Phoebe, a leopard gecko that he loved more than anything else in the world.

I had never worked with anyone who had such significant autism before and found that his writing reflected his inability to gauge appropriate social distances. In that sense, he qualified as an "inappropriate communicator," but that problem was significantly mitigated by the fact that there was something so likable and earnest about this young man that his story promised to be quite moving.

So I cut. And cut. And cut. The drafts came in at four or five times longer than they were supposed to, and there was a definite feeling of his standing too close to me and saying too much. Torrents of emotion went on for pages, and it was evident that he had very little concept of how neurotypical people communicate their feelings. But, again, he had something to say, so ultimately he was able to bring the essay home. He wrote about the lizard's shedding of its skin and his own "shedding of the skin he was born with" in order to assume a persona that helped him function in the mainstream world.

When I first talked to him about this concept of communicating with his reader, I wasn't sure how far he could go with it, as the dynamic of interpersonal communication was essentially foreign to him. He understood, however, that this was something that could be learned — and, being the good student he was, he learned it.

## Identifying Your Reader

Back in 1972, I graduated from Johns Hopkins University with a baccalaureate degree in English literature. I then decided to stay on for another year to earn a master's degree in a program called Writing Seminars. That year was significant for me, as it gave me some space and financial support as I developed my identity as a writer. Upon graduation, I went to work for a few years in publishing in New York City; since then, for the rest of my life, I have made my living, such as it has been in any given year, as a freelance writer. There have been full-time jobs here and there in the world of film, but those have just been drops in the bucket. As a freelance writer, I have learned to write in many different disciplines, so I could help support my family and generally survive in a tough world.

Earlier in my career, I did my best to earn my living by writing books. I always had a rich creative project going, such as a novel, and wrote quickie books on the side for money. The latter ranged from pseudonymous historical romances to pseudonymous young adult ghost stories. Whatever. If it helped to pay the bills, I wrote it. The logistics of depending on publishers' advances proved a nightmare, however, as I would sometimes have to wait months to get a check that was due me. So I realized, better late than never, that I needed a more secure way to earn a living.

My life changed when I became what is fancily called a "higher-education marketing communications consultant." That means that I wrote all kinds of materials for colleges and universities, from recruitment brochures to donor solicitations to departmental web pages. The very first thing I did when I sat down to work on a new project was to ask myself who my audience would be. Would it be a sixteen- or seventeen-year-old high school student thinking seriously about college for the first time? Would it be a parent about to send a child off to a very expensive university? Would it be a prospective graduate student? Would it be a recent alum, out in the workforce for ten years or less? Or would it be an older alum, well-heeled and well-cushioned, seated in the plush library of a stately home?

When I had that potential reader clearly in mind, the writing could start. I wouldn't even think about outlining a piece until I had that face in front of me. Everything about the piece — the rhythm, the tone, the structure — would be influenced by that face.

You would be surprised how many people go into a writing situation without paying any attention to the important step of identifying the audience. A few years back, I went to a retirement luncheon for an anesthesiologist friend of mine — let's call him Edward — who had been with his hospital for forty years. His fellow physician — let's call him Ralph — delivered some remarks. (The names are fictitious to protect the innocent.) Now, it is understood that public speaking is agonizing for most people, but oral delivery wasn't Ralph's worst problem. In fact, he was clearly well-meaning and had a pleasant presence. The problem was that he was talking about Edward as if no one in the room knew him:

> In the thirty years that Edward and I have worked together, I have always known him to be a responsible and conscientious professional who gives 100 percent to whatever he undertakes. Edward is organized, resourceful, and devotes painstaking attention to even the most minor details. Edward never disappoints. If he tells you he is going to do something, he will do it.

(This is verbatim, mind you. I was so struck by Ralph's remarks that I asked if I could get a copy, thinking I might be able to make use of them someday. Naturally, he was very flattered.) Ralph went on, addressing the guests as if they were a review panel, there to determine whether Edward was a good candidate for an open position, rather than as a room full of friends, family, and coworkers who had gathered to honor him and wish him well.

One of the best things insecure public speakers can do is to make eye contact with audience members one by one. That may be a bit hard to do with a large audience, in which case they'll want to pick out select members with whom to have that special eye contact, but I've taken that suggestion even further. When I do a book presentation for a small group — let's say twenty-five people or so — I will go over and introduce myself to people as they enter the room. This shocks and delights them, and before we're even out of the gate, we've connected.

Ralph should have kept that tip in mind when he was

preparing his remarks. He should have visualized all who had gathered for this bittersweet event: the other partners, the support staff, the ex-patients, and Edward's family members. In doing so, he would have seen that there were real people in the room who had real connections to Edward, and surely he could have found some appealing anecdotes that would have attested to Edward's qualities — his resourcefulness, his conscientiousness, his attention to detail — without merely listing them like attributes in a letter of reference. He would have been able to concentrate on the human thread that should always be kept in mind when engaged in communication, the idea that someone — some *one* — will be reading or listening to what you have written.

To identify your reader, start by asking such questions as:

- How old?
- How educated?
- How conservative?
- How liberal?
- How globalized?
- How affluent?
- How concerned about the issue you're writing about?
- How familiar with your material?
- How interested in your material?
- How much attention available to devote to you?
- How set in his or her ways?

This is just a sampling of questions; there may be many more. You don't have to answer all of them, but by attempting to answer some, you will have a better chance of focusing your writing, and that will be helpful to you and to your audience.

## Your Contract with the Reader

This agreement is made between the writer (the "Writer") and the reader (the "Reader").

WHEREAS the Writer is the sole owner and conveyor of the writing;

WHEREAS the Reader is the recipient of the writing;

NOW, THEREFORE, in consideration of the above and the mutual covenants, terms, conditions, and restrictions contained herein, the parties hereto declare and agree as follows...

What you see above is politely referred to as "legal language," which you must be sure to avoid in your writing (unless you are in fact a lawyer). We will discuss the pitfalls of legal language later in the book when we focus on jargon, but for now just know that we want to avoid, at all costs, words like *aforesaid*, *prior to*, *in the event of*, *terminate*, and so on. There is actually some kind of movement (probably a mini movement) in the legal community to advance the cause of "plain-language legal writing," which means language that is clear and comprehensible to any reader. Wouldn't that be lovely? In any event, this is our moment to focus on something that is at least quasi-legalistic: the writer's contract with the reader.

Such a contract is implicit, not explicit. Obviously, when we finish a piece of writing and deliver it to the reader, we do not ask that person to sign on the dotted line, absolving us for any mistakes we may have made. We do not require the reader to read the entirety of what has been delivered, nor do we demand that he or she *somehow* demonstrate an understanding of what has been read. When it comes to the implicit contract, however, there is much at stake.

The burden of responsibility in this contract falls primarily on you, the writer, rather than on the reader. You have no control over the reader, so there's not all that much you can ask of the reader. You can hope that he will devote attention to what you've written, but if the reader's bathtub overflows, the reality is that his attention will be diverted and for who knows how long. The good news, however, is that if you provide your reader with something sufficiently captivating, he will gladly give you his attention. Very few people manage to fall asleep while reading Edgar Allan Poe's "The Pit and the Pendulum," J. D. Salinger's *The Catcher in the Rye*, or Erik Larson's *The Devil in the White City*.

When you consider your contract with the reader, it's best to approach it as a kind of "Bill of Rights" assuring the reader that your writing will have certain basic qualities. Let's think of these qualities as the six *C*s:

1. **Clarity.** Everything in your piece should be as clear as can be. That doesn't mean you have to completely forgo ambiguity, which can be a powerful tool in certain kinds of writing, but it does mean that, sentence to sentence and paragraph to paragraph, you should strive to be as clear as possible. Ambiguity only works

if you understand the point of your own writing. Ambiguity is not synonymous with confusion.

2.  **Conciseness.** Generally speaking, readers are stingy with their time. Everyone has a lot to do these days, and when a reader is given something to read, the implicit understanding — that is, the implicit *contract* — stipulates that the Writer (you) will not waste the Reader's time. In other words, fewer words. Fewer adjectives, fewer adverbs, fewer metaphors, and more clean, muscular prose. And keep in mind that faulty punctuation also takes up the reader's time — what is that comma doing there? — which is why everything must be pored over carefully.

3.  **Construction.** It is no real stretch to compare a piece of writing to a piece of cabinetry. Both demand a high level of functionality, an appreciation for aesthetics, a good finish, and clean lines. Those clean lines are part of your contract with the reader. We can't expect a reader to jump all over the place, trying to keep pace with the random shifts of the writer's thought processes. When you are telling a story — which oftentimes you are, even if what you are writing doesn't seem like a story — then you must be aware that what is going on in your mind is not necessarily being conveyed to your reader. If you start out in one location in the first paragraph and wind up in another location in the second paragraph, the reader will want to know how you got there. That's called "tracking" — and it's a writing issue that many writers tend to ignore.

4. **Color.** You, the writer, must do your best to create a piece of writing that feels vivid and fully drawn. Bland, colorless writing goes down like cold porridge, while overcooked writing, screaming with verbal sound effects, is as hard to swallow as Sriracha on four-alarm chili. Finding a palette that works for you (and this needn't be and probably shouldn't be the same palette for everything you write) will play an important role in determining if your writing is successful. You have many colored pencils in your box. The key is to find which ones work for you — an issue we will be taking up in detail as we go forward.

5. **Courtesy.** DO YOU KNOW WHAT I MEAN BY *COURTESY?* If you're familiar with email courtesy, then you know that the sentence I just wrote, entirely in capital letters, is called "shouting." People don't like to be shouted at — it feels discourteous — and so an email in all caps is a no-no. Think about ways that you, the writer, might be discourteous to your reader. Persuasive writing, for example, should not be peppered with exclamation points as you try to make your points. (E.g., "Dear Sir or Madam, I was infuriated to discover that the squeegee I ordered from you did not work! I would have expected more, given your Amazon reviews!") Sarcasm, snarky comments, arch expressions, especially those in a foreign language (*Comme ça!*), are all ways to alienate the reader — and an alienated reader is tremendously difficult to reel back in. Remember, readers can find many other things to do with their time instead of reading what you have written.

6. **Commitment.** Of our six *C*s, commitment is probably the most difficult one to get a bead on. We understand readily what it means to be courteous, concise, and clear, but when we say that a writer needs to be "committed," what are we suggesting? By commitment, we mean that you will try to make your piece the very best it can be. If it takes eight drafts to get a piece right, even a short one, so be it. It's not done until it's done. And the issue of commitment brings us to the contract that writers have with themselves.

## Your Contract with the Writer (Yourself)

As we've said, when you set out to write, you enter into an implicit contract with your reader. Let's further examine your end of the deal and consider the issue of discipline. If you bring certain habits to your writing, your chances of staying with the work and improving at it increase exponentially. George Orwell wrote:

> A scrupulous writer, in every sentence that he writes, will ask himself at least four questions, thus:
>
> 1. What am I trying to say?
> 2. What words will express it?
> 3. What image or idiom will make it clearer?
> 4. Is this image fresh enough to have an effect?
>
> And he will probably ask himself two more:
>
> 1. Could I put it more shortly?
> 2. Have I said anything that is avoidably ugly?

Orwell's remarks strike me as quite wonderful, and they align with what I have written about your contract with the reader. That is to say, Orwell is talking about the issues of clarity, conciseness, and color that we have identified. "But I'm not looking to be a *scrupulous* writer," I hear you protesting. Okay. I understand that not everyone is cut out to be as scrupulous a writer as Orwell, but even so, all writers should aspire to the standards they set for themselves.

Let's use the word *rigor*, shall we? It's a buzzword in educational circles these days, but it is often misused and misunderstood. Rigor is about learning at a high level and becoming truly engaged in your learning. In that sense, I like the application of the word *rigor* to the writing process as we have been describing it.

It is important to understand, right from day one, that writing requires rigorous work. Writing doesn't come easily to professional writers, and it won't come easily to you. That needn't be a problem, however. A lot of things in life don't come easily, like a good golf game or graceful ballroom dancing, but we're willing to work at those things. Similarly, we need to be willing to work at our writing to bring it along to higher levels — and the results, when we do that work, are soon apparent. Many writing problems are rather simple and technical in nature, and those can be ironed out easily enough. When some of those problems start to fall away, your confidence will increase, and greater confidence will lead to greater overall fluidity and control in your writing.

Rigor starts to kick in as well when you begin to recognize that writing is a knowable process and that your drafts are a critical component of that process. We will discuss the drafting process in detail when we come to Step Five, but for now it is important to remind ourselves that *every* piece of writing should go through as many drafts as necessary to get it right. An email may take only one draft — but if you don't like spelling mistakes in your emails (as I don't), then it will likely take more than one draft. More demanding writing projects will inevitably require more drafts.

It is important to understand that the drafting process is not simply a matter of heaping draft upon draft, with no particular logic or design. Each draft has a focus and a purpose, and when you understand that, as you will by the end of this book, you can then work more effectively and with a better chance of fulfilling that contract with yourself.

## The Relearning Curve

In the Introduction, I brought up the idea of "relearning" how to write. I compared it to the concepts that underlie the Feldenkrais Method, which helps people with musculoskeletal issues "relearn" how to move. With regard to writing, we might even take this concept a step farther to suggest that some people need to "unlearn" how to write. Too many of us were taught to write in ways that felt like drudgery. There were too many rules, now recognized as outdated and obsolete, and far too much emphasis on mistakes. *Rigor* and *rigidity* are not synonymous, and too many of us grew up (or are growing up right now) in an atmosphere in which writing is taught rigidly and thus ineffectively.

I won't say that writing is as natural as eating, drinking, or sleeping, but I will say that writing should never feel unnatural. Nor should writing be something that is available only to certain people. When you develop the conviction that you can express yourself clearly and persuasively in a piece of writing, then you will feel a sense of empowerment that is revelatory. You can make your wishes and opinions known without expressing anger, neediness, or any other emotion that gets in the way of your message. You will be able to concentrate on what you want to say, and you will be able to say it, which is a profoundly satisfying feeling.

In 1839, the immensely popular English novelist, playwright, poet, and politician Edward Bulwer-Lytton, who coined the now laughable opening line, "It was a dark and stormy night," introduced another catchphrase in his play *Richelieu: or, The Conspiracy*. "The pen is mightier than the sword," says the cardinal in act 2, scene 2, and so one of the most long-lived clichés in our language was born. Cliché or not, the thought remains apt. The pen — that is, written language — gives those who know how to wield it an unmatched sense of power and confidence. And everyone should have a piece of that.

Sometimes when I am working with a group of writers, I will ask them to think back on their history with writing and answer a few questions:

- How do you feel when you sit down to write something?
- Have you ever been told that you write well?
- Have you ever been told that you don't write well?
- Do you feel able to assess what you have written?

• If you could change something about your writing,
   what would it be?

To the first question, I often get answers like, "I feel nervous," "I feel confused," or even "I feel sick." It is altogether natural to feel nervous and even a bit nauseous when we sit down to write something. It's called performance anxiety, and everyone experiences some aspect of it when confronting a blank sheet of paper or computer screen.

One immediately reassuring thing to remember is that we live in an age when we are lucky enough to have easy and abundant resources that can resolve small technical writing issues. Say you don't know whether to use *proportionate* or *proportional* in a sentence. All you have to do is google "proportionate vs. proportional," and you'll get your answer. Knowing that such resources exist can free writers up to "not sweat the small stuff," as the cliché goes. (And more about clichés when we get to Step Six.) So as we relearn our writing, that feeling that afflicts all of us at the beginning of an assignment — naked fear — will become far more manageable.

I have asked many, many people if they have ever been told that they write well, and I have yet to find someone who has answered yes. Most people, after all, don't write especially *well*. To write well, it helps to have a natural gift, and natural gifts, whether they are bestowed on dancers, tennis players, mathematicians, or writers, are few and far between. That said, a great many people have managed to become perfectly competent writers, but they may never have been praised for that skill.

When people are asked if they have been told that they

don't write well, many hands usually go up. I see evidence of such ego abuse all the time, all over the place. A year ago, I worked with an enormously bright high-school senior at a top preparatory school in New York City. Following the precepts I use in my work, this student wrote a wonderful college-admission essay about performing magic tricks on a hospital floor for chronically ill children, during which time he came to the realization that medicine, his career aspiration, was not magic.

It was an unusual, complex, and frank essay, but his college counselor, who was notoriously authoritarian in her somewhat misguided convictions, did not understand this kind of essay and pushed him in a far more conventional direction. That would have been bad enough, but she also told him that *he didn't know how to write*. Now, here was a very gifted young man in a top private school who was being told he didn't know how to write — when he most certainly did. Just imagine how many less-privileged people get told such things day in and day out.

As to our fourth question — Do you feel able to assess what you have written? — most people report that they do not. Their experience, by and large, is that when they write something, it is then put out there for a thumbs-up or thumbs-down reaction. They lack an understanding of self-editing, of how to bring a piece of writing through a series of drafts, of how to achieve some critical distance from what they have written so that they can make changes large and small.

And when it comes to that last question — If you could change something about your writing, what would it be? — most people unfortunately seem to focus on the small stuff.

"I'd like to be a better speller," some will say, remembering back to those very simple days of their youth when good writing seemed to be synonymous with good spelling and somehow forgetting that we now have that eminently useful tool called spellchecker. Others long to have "good grammar" or "good vocabulary." Hey, let's hear it for good spelling, good grammar, and good vocabulary, but it's a problem when we view writing as something for which there is a quick and simple fix instead of as a discipline that grows as we grow with it. When we incorporate writing into our lives in an ongoing way, then we can begin to access the pleasure and power that are connected with it.

## The Discipline of Writing

Writing does require discipline, and applying oneself to a writing task demands a certain amount of willpower. After all, there are many easier ways to occupy one's time, whether it's watching television, reading John Grisham, going out to brunch, you name it. Here, however, we are talking about writing as a *discipline*, or "area of study."

Here's a thought: let's finally dispense with the idea of writing as that thing we had to do back in school that we weren't very good at. Let's instead think of it as something that we are motivated to learn and improve at. In that respect, we can compare it to learning a foreign language. We want to learn Italian, because soon we will be visiting Rome and we think it would be fun to be able to say, "*Si prega di passare il calamaro* (Please pass the squid)."

We want to be able to feel comfortable and empowered

when we are sitting in that trattoria and so, in order to develop some sense of facility with Italian, we are willing to set aside time each day — in the car, over coffee in the morning, instead of watching Netflix at night — to do the work of learning this language. We don't make ourselves crazy, though, because we know that we may never be able to speak Italian like Marcello Mastroianni, but we tell ourselves that this is something that we want to do, something that we can integrate into our busy life, and something that we will improve at as time goes by.

Why can't writing be like that?

The answer is that it can be exactly like that. It's time now to stop thinking about writing as an either/or — "right or wrong" or "good or bad" — endeavor, but rather to think of it as an activity that you can work at as time permits and one that you will get better at, the more you do it.

You can begin to bring writing into your life with small exercises that needn't take more than ten minutes at a pop. And, again, there is no right or wrong here — just opportunities to use a muscle that has gone unused for too long. Here are some ideas for those small exercises:

- Write a "still life" of a fruit or vegetable. Place the object on a table and describe it.
- Explain to somebody from Mars how to tie a shoelace.
- Think of a joke you like and then write it up. See if you can make someone (even yourself) laugh.
- Write a review of a TV episode (a film is probably too ambitious).
- Write up a dream.

- Think of a job you could never imagine yourself getting and then write a cover letter to apply for it.
- Leave a letter of instruction to a house sitter on how to take care of your pet or plant.
- Write a "self-portrait" describing your face.
- Write a letter to the editor explaining why _____ (fill in the blank) should not be permitted in your neighborhood.
- Write a codicil to your will leaving a certain possession to a certain person. Explain what it is and why you're doing it.
- Write a letter home from someplace you've never been.
- Imagine that you are a restaurant reviewer and describe a dish you have enjoyed (or not enjoyed).

Don't feel compelled to do any or all of these — or you might do some and then make up some exercises of your own and see how they go. The idea is to get yourself writing in a way that feels free and maybe even fun. Since these small exercises are for your eyes only, you will not have to worry about "right or wrong" or "good or bad," because those words don't apply here.

But without value judgments, you are wondering, how you will assess yourself? Well, you won't assess yourself — yet. Like a Sunday painter who goes out *en plein air* on a beautiful day, you'll do what you're doing purely for the sake of enjoyment and for building up skills. And you may find yourself surprised by your efforts. You may find that waves of energy begin to pulse through your writing. When describing that peach on the table, for example, where did you pull the word *succulent* from? You didn't even realize you knew that word.

Writing a self-portrait of your face? Aren't you surprised by your ability to limn your physiognomy and capture the moods that are reflected in your eyes, on your skin, in the twist of your mouth?

Writing that codicil to your will? You never realized until this moment how much you wanted your friend Robert to have that wine gourd you bought when the two of you traveled to Spain years ago. Writing this short codicil has allowed you to capture a shared moment that was very special and, as well, the tenor of a friendship that has survived beyond most.

It is far easier to enter into the discipline of writing when less is at stake. What we are trying to do is to establish a habit that gets built up through practice. Something that you've been doing your best to avoid suddenly becomes something that feels available to you. Suddenly, writing feels like a natural form of communication, and you soon discover that you can try it out all over the place.

## Suspending Judgment

Remember, we are not going to pass judgment on ourselves as writers — not on day 1, or on day 4, or on day 104 or 1,004. It is one thing to be discerning — discernment is a critical part of self-editing — but passing judgment on yourself and telling yourself that you are not a good writer have no constructive place in the writing process.

Too many people are more than willing to pass judgment

on others' writing, and that's just a fact of life. When we put our writing out into the world, the expectation is that it is going to be "reviewed," and reviews can often be quite harsh. Just google "bad reviews of great books," and some real howlers will immediately pop up. Here, for instance, is what the *New York Times* had to say about Vladimir Nabokov's *Lolita*, one of the great books of our time, when it was first published:

> *Lolita*, then, is undeniably news in the world of books. Unfortunately, it is bad news. There are two equally serious reasons why it isn't worth any adult reader's attention. The first is that it is dull, dull, dull in a pretentious, florid and archly fatuous fashion. The second is that it is repulsive.

All right. So much for the *New York Times*. How about the *Atlantic* on Walt Whitman's *Leaves of Grass*?

> It is no discredit to Walt Whitman that he wrote *Leaves of Grass*, only that he did not burn it afterwards.

So, as I say, writers do not need to beat themselves up when there is always somebody around to do it for them. The learning process goes much better when we treat ourselves with dignity and respect and give ourselves time to accommodate our learning pace, whatever that might be, to the task.

In any case, soon enough — in fact, by the end of this seven-step program — you should begin to see stirrings of improvement in your writing, and there will be little reason to berate yourself. All the things you used to say about yourself — "I can't write," "I can't think on paper," "I can't make a decent sentence," "I can't spell," "I can't punctuate" — will begin to fall away, and everything will become that much clearer.

## Up Close

At the end of each of these seven steps, we are going to examine a piece of text in light of some of the issues we have been talking about. In this Up Close exercise, we will be looking at the opening paragraph of a college admission essay by a student I recently had the pleasure of working with.

I say "pleasure," because this student was an extremely bright young woman who worked very hard at everything she took on — although perhaps too hard at her writing. The daughter of Chinese immigrants, she was born in the United States. A gifted STEM (science, technology, engineering, and mathematics) major, she wanted to combine her interest in genetics with her entrepreneurial goals. She was enormously excited about the prospect of studying at a fine institution, and she deserved to go to a top college — but she had to get past the stumbling block of the admission essay.

My student's biggest problem is that she had no idea how to tell a story. We're going to look at the art of storytelling when we get to Step Three, because, as I said earlier, you would be surprised to see how much storytelling goes on in our writing, even when we least expect it. This student's approach to her essay was to pack it with information about herself and her achievements. Her achievements were indeed significant, but she had no sense that a story demands a certain kind of rhythm.

In fact, she had an interesting enough story to tell, which concerned an encounter she had on a city street with a homeless person. I knew we would have our work cut out for us, however, when I saw the opening paragraph of her first draft:

> Blaring cars, rushing people, and SEPTA buses embrace me as I exit the platform of the train. A homeless person stands in front of this blurring image. I see homeless people every day. The desperate look, the tattered clothes and oversized shoes, and the emaciated hand are common reoccurrences. Memories of my mother advising me to stay away from strangers flood my mind. This time, however, I approached closer and found that the middle-aged homeless man was reading a frayed book. Dropping a few coins in a tiny paper cup, he looked at me gratefully. His eyes darted back to the novel. I was amazed. He loved reading. The book reflected my home away from home — the library.

Right away, I could tell that she had some difficulty articulating her thoughts. Let's look at that opening sentence:

> Blaring cars, rushing people, and SEPTA buses embrace me as I exit the platform of the train.

"Do you see any problems with that sentence?" I remember asking her. She did not.

"Do blaring cars and SEPTA buses have the capacity to embrace people?" I asked. She conceded the point, and we went on.

A homeless person stands in front of this blurring image. I see homeless people every day. The desperate look, the tattered clothes and oversized shoes, and the emaciated hand are common reoccurrences.

There were changes that needed to be made here as well, I pointed out. For instance, "oversized shoes" connote circus clowns rather than homeless people. "Emaciated hand"? I didn't think so. It sounded somewhat maudlin.

We went on:

Memories of my mother advising me to stay away from strangers flood my mind. This time, however, I approached closer and found that the middle-aged homeless man was reading a frayed book. Dropping a few coins in a tiny paper cup, he looked at me gratefully.

You may have noticed some tense inconsistencies running throughout this piece ("Memories...flood my mind" is present tense, while "I approached closer" is past tense). I see such tense issues all the time. They are especially prevalent among writers who are not native speakers or who live among nonnative speakers, but they can certainly appear as well in the writing of people whose ancestors came over on the *Mayflower*.

The most problematic sentence, however, was that last one: "Dropping a few coins in a tiny paper cup, he looked at me gratefully." Had my student kept in mind the good advice to start a sentence with a noun or a verb, she would not have gotten tripped up there. In fact, she was the one dropping the coins in the paper cup, but as the sentence reads the coin dropper was the homeless man. She ultimately digested the lesson on starting sentences with a noun or a verb, and her writing started to improve as a result.

And then there was that last section:

> His eyes darted back to the novel. I was amazed. He loved reading. The book reflected my home away from home — the library.

That very last sentence — "The book reflected my home away from home — the library" — is a good example of the kind of sentence that may mean something to the writer, but has no meaning for the reader. Books don't reflect libraries, and something much more pointed than that was needed to introduce this first big thought in the essay.

There were times when this student's writing made me hang my head in despair, but, as I have described her, she also happened to be a gifted learner. She loved to learn and loved to read. (Her love of reading was a big part of her essay.) She worked closely with me, in the kind of extremely productive collaborative relationship that can be generated between a writer and an editor, each giving and taking, and so we were able to bring her essay to a very good place. It never became, nor could it ever become, the kind of essay that a truly gifted writer can produce, but that's not a problem. It became a very good essay indeed, compared to what most people produce.

Here is how that problematic first paragraph resolved itself:

> Car horns, bus fumes, and the rush of morning commuters greet me as I exit the subway. Walking along the street, I see a homeless person up ahead, camped out

on the sidewalk. The desperate look, the tattered garments, and the outstretched hand are common sights on this daily route. This time, however, as I come closer, I can see that the homeless man — middle-aged with unruly blond hair — is reading a book. I stop for a moment, so unexpected is this sight, and, when I drop a few coins into the paper cup he is holding, he looks at me gratefully until finally his eyes dart back to the novel. I am amazed. He loves reading. So do I.

As you can see, we fixed the embracing buses and cars and made some other alterations at the top, like changing "emaciated hand" to "outstretched hand" (no point laying it on so thick). Treating the homeless man as a significant character in the piece, we gave him some physical detail and clarified who was dropping coins into the cup. We also stressed the feeling of empathy and connection centered on reading at the end of that paragraph, which piques interest and will be our lead-in to the next paragraph.

All of this was the usual kind of work that any writer engages in, but it was especially gratifying to see my student's commitment to the process. She was excited to watch her piece evolve, to see its architecture come through, and to polish her work to a fine sheen. She came to understand that communicating with your reader is the essence of writing, and she approached her work not with the trepidation that had previously accompanied her efforts, so confused was she about the mechanics of writing, but rather with a sense of rigor that allowed her to get where she needed to go. She diligently held up her end of the contract and was rewarded with a very solid essay.

## ROUNDUP

1. Writing is all about communication, and you can communicate more effectively when you identify, or at least visualize, your reader.
2. There are many ways to be an ineffective communicator — you can be insecure, inconsiderate, inappropriate, inaccessible, inexact — and those problems can exist simultaneously.
3. You can help to identify your reader by asking questions about that person. Is he or she young or old? Conservative or liberal? Affluent? Educated? Familiar or unfamiliar with your material?
4. As a writer, you enter into an implicit contract with your reader, promising that you will be clear, concise, committed, and courteous and that you will offer solid construction and well-drawn color.
5. As a writer, you also enter into an implicit contract with yourself. You promise to approach your writing with a sense of rigor.
6. You may need to relearn or unlearn aspects of your writing.
7. Short writing exercises that you can integrate easily into your life will help you develop the discipline of writing.
8. You promise to suspend judgment upon yourself as a writer.

## STEP TWO

## Gear Up

In Step One, we talked about that frightening sensation of being in alien territory that many people feel when they sit down to write. To temper that fear, we identified the idea of *communication* as a stabilizing element that can help you understand, at its core, what writing is all about. Writing *is* communication — which is a revelation for many people who may have no difficulty communicating verbally, but who feel frustrated when it comes to writing.

We also talked about the implicit contract between writer and reader that lies at the very heart of writing. Understanding and accepting this contract will allow you to move away from the idea that writing is an overwhelming and amorphous endeavor. Instead, you will begin to view it as stimulating and even invigorating work that has structure and purpose and that can be learned.

Now, in this second step — Gear Up — we are going to

further demystify the act of writing by focusing on the actual problems, big and small, that interfere with the writing process, particularly at the outset. These problems afflict all writers, but of course the intensity varies. For those who have consecrated their lives to the act of writing, as great writers do, the agony and the ecstasy are naturally amplified. For the rest of us, the discomfort may be brief or intermittent, but still agonizing.

## Staring, Squirming, and Shuffling

If you should ever have the opportunity to study people through a one-way mirror as they launch themselves into the act of writing, you would surely witness some odd behaviors. Hair twirling, finger cracking, and all kinds of nervous gestures give way to walking around in circles, bouncing balls, stretching arms and legs, and ultimately to abdominal crunches, flossing, and I don't know what else. Then, when some of that nervous energy has been expended, it's time to go back to the desk and the dreaded blank page or screen. A few more sentences or maybe even a paragraph or two are squeezed out, and then the vicious cycle starts all over again. By the end of the work session, the stress has taken its toll, so is it any wonder that so many famous writers were alcoholics? (Edgar Allan Poe, Dorothy Parker, William Faulkner, Carson McCullers, and James Joyce, to name a few.)

The lives and destinies of those famous folks depended on their writing, so when their words were not forthcoming, they had reason to turn to drink. For the lay writer, however, it is good to know that all that staring, squirming, and shuffling is simply part of the process. And what, you may wonder, is fueling all of that?

By and large, the answer is fear.

When we write, we are engaged in the act of bringing together vision and execution, and our fear is commensurate with the scope of our undertaking. If we are writing an email to a friend, for instance, we are undertaking something very nonthreatening, so our fear level is minimal. When we are applying to a job, however, and we're writing an email that will serve as the cover letter for a résumé we are attaching, there is a great deal more at stake, so the fear factor spikes. When we sit down to write an important paper for a course we're taking, a toast for a wedding at which we are playing a central role, a letter to an editor regarding a cause about which we feel impassioned, or, raising the stakes ever so much higher, a novel with which we're hoping to make our mark in the world, the fear factor rises exponentially and the act of sitting down to write becomes increasingly stressful.

Years ago, a friend gave me a present of a small plaque on which was inscribed these words from Douglas Adams, author of the humor classic *The Hitchhiker's Guide to the Galaxy*: "Writing is easy. You only need to stare at a piece of paper until your forehead bleeds." One of history's greatest writers, Johann Wolfgang von Goethe, had similar words of caution: "If you think about writing while you're writing, you'll go mad. Think about it later when tidying up." (My problem has often been that I tidy up while I'm writing, but that's just a form of procrastination, which we will discuss momentarily.) So it is safe to say that fear features in the life of any writer — or, at the very least, features into any act of writing.

It's good to put that statement out there, because it legitimizes the fear, making us feel less inadequate and more realistic about the challenges of the work. We know we will make mistakes, and we know we will be far less than perfect, but let's also remember the words of Robert Cormier, author of the young adult classic *The Chocolate War*, who said, "The beautiful part of writing is that you don't have to get it right the first time, unlike, say, brain surgery." In other words, we're not going to kill anyone with our awkward first, second, or third draft.

## That Old Devil Procrastination

Even if you recognize how closely fear is linked to writing, don't assume that such recognition on its own is going to protect you when you sit down before your blank computer screen or sheet of paper. That's when procrastination often rears its dreaded head.

Procrastination is a remarkably powerful force that, if left uncontrolled, can sweep all your best intentions away and leave you feeling guilty and anxious. It's also a force that is present in the lives of all those who write. In fact, the brilliant comic writer Paul Rudnick has said, "Writing is 90 percent procrastination: reading magazines, eating cereal out of the box, watching infomercials."

Procrastination has become even more of a demon in our current age, when we sit at the computer and an entire universe of distraction awaits us on the internet. In fact, the film director Noah Baumbach has said, "When you find yourself on the internet when you're supposed to be writing, you've already lost."

It's true. These days, you may find yourself working away, developing some sense of energy, and then you google a word to make sure you're using it correctly, and the next thing you know you're down the YouTube rabbit hole, watching last night's Colbert monologue or a cat doing its business on a potty. Or else you're emailing or checking the sports scores or seeing what is going on in Washington or exploring any number of diversions that are always there, lying in wait, ready to whisk you away from the task at hand. The good news, however, is that there are reliable ways to keep procrastination at bay.

People who are curious about a writer's life often ask me what my writing schedule is like. They seem to want to hear that I get up in the morning, work for four hours, and then, enviably, have the rest of the day to myself. Or perhaps they suspect that I work through the night, like some romantic hybrid of Percy Bysshe Shelley and Jack Kerouac. In fact, although a strict and prescribed schedule might work very well for any number of writers, I rely instead on the quota system. That is to say, on any given day that I designate as a workday (and not all days are; I believe in weekends, even for writers), I set myself a quota that must be met before that day is over. The word count on the quota is entirely variable. It could be 100 words or it could be 1,000. Writer's choice — and it often depends on the project I am working on.

Let me give you an example of how I use the quota system with my students. If I see that someone is stuck on an essay, even if it's just 650 words long, I will suggest a quota. "Don't go to sleep tonight until you've squeezed out 50 words," I will say. And if the writer follows my advice, she will come to see that even a mere 50 words, good or bad, is a powerful weapon against that rotten feeling that procrastination engenders.

As we all know, procrastination is not a behavior that is in any way restricted to writing. (You should see me avoiding my income-tax preparation.) It can rear its head whenever and wherever you are looking to avoid a task. Simply put, procrastination is the act of putting off until tomorrow what you can do today.

Procrastination generally leads to shame and guilt, but take heart in knowing that just about everyone procrastinates at some point or another. Take heart too in knowing that there are other specific strategies, in addition to the quota system, that can help pull you out of the procrastination trap.

As you may know, a motivator can be extrinsic (coming from the outside) or intrinsic (coming from within). As a professional writer, I have always had a clear extrinsic motivator in view: the need to make money. Whenever I sold a book, I would get half of the advance on signing and half on delivery and acceptance of the manuscript. The fact that my family depended on realizing the rest of my income from that last half of the advance was one heck of a good extrinsic motivator. I also had intrinsic motivations to call upon: my desire to succeed, my interest in my craft, my sense of professional responsibility.

When you find yourself procrastinating, it is useful to identify the motivators that will help you do the work. Having a hard time writing that cover letter to accompany your résumé? Combat the procrastination by telling yourself that you need that job (external motivator) and you will have no chance if you don't get that letter done. Although that might momentarily ramp up the sense of anxiety that fueled the procrastination in the first place, that anxiety will likely subside, and the clarity that comes with identifying an objective may be enough to get you over the hump.

And, once again, don't forget that quota system. Producing your prescribed allotment — 50 words, 100 words, 200 words, whatever you choose — is going to leave you feeling virtuous instead of rotten. But 50 words is nothing to get excited about, you protest. It is, if you've been stuck — 50 words are better than zero words, after all — and ultimately you'll see how 50 words can lead to 100 words and then to 200 words, and soon you have some critical mass to work with. Once you're starting to feel more confident about your ability to produce, you can raise your daily quota from 50 to 100 or 200 or 500 words.

Another way to combat procrastination is to set deadlines for yourself. In fact, many of my college applicants plead with me for deadlines. The freedom of being without one is confusing to them and sometimes even paralyzing. As a professional writer, I can certainly relate to the power of the deadline. In fact, deadlines have "inspired" me when all else has failed. Of course, common sense dictates that deadlines become meaningless if they are set too far in advance. If you are writing a 200-word essay and set your deadline a month away, that essentially counts for nothing.

One other thought regarding procrastination. If you've set yourself a quota for the day (let's say 500 words), there could still be a problem with ignition. One way you can deal with that is by giving yourself a very small goal at the outset. Tell yourself that you will not move until you write the first sentence (even though first sentences are especially difficult to pull off). Tell yourself that you will not move until you create a rudimentary outline for the piece. Tell yourself you will not move until you get down some brainstorming notes (to be explained). Writer's choice.

## Getting Started

Now that we have addressed some of the psychological impediments that can hinder the act of writing, let's focus on ways that will help us as we get to work. A good way to begin is by creating a plan — and a good way to start on a plan is to ask questions.

Writers and questions go hand in hand. For the most part, writers are a curious bunch who want to find out as much as they can about the world and its inhabitants. In fact, many writers come to realize that they can be comfortable in almost any social situation simply by asking people questions about themselves. Generally, people are very happy to talk about themselves, so asking a simple leading question like, "What do you do?" or "Where did you grow up?" will break the ice effectively.

Similarly, by asking questions of yourself, you can break the ice with your writing task. Imagine yourself seated at your desk, staring at a blank screen or sheet of paper and feeling utterly lost. What is your best next move? Try formulating some key questions and answer them to the best of your ability.

Here are the kinds of questions I ask myself when I sit down to write something, whether it's a ten-minute play, a fundraising brochure for a university alumni/ae association, or a personal essay that I hope might evolve into an op-ed piece in a newspaper:

- What am I looking to say?
- How can I best communicate my message?
- What do I want readers to know and understand when they finish reading what I have written?
- What can I do to capture my readers' attention?
- Do I understand my raw material?
- Am I looking to persuade? To argue? To amuse? Or some combination thereof?
- Which part of this writing task do I feel confident about?
- Which part of this writing task feels overwhelming to me?
- What can I do to break up the overwhelming parts into more manageable components?

Keep in mind that you don't have to ask yourself every one of these questions at the outset of a writing project. You may decide to ask only a few that seem particularly relevant to what you are setting out to do.

Take note as well that you needn't have all the answers to these questions at the beginning of the writing process. After all, the writing process is largely a matter of discovery, and your drafts are designed to encourage that discovery. For instance, the answer to the question, "What can I do to capture my readers' attention?" might not become evident until you're into your third or fourth draft. Then you tell yourself, "Eureka! I see now that a bold structural move, like starting my piece with the ending and working up to it, is the answer to that question. I was simply being too linear and hence too formulaic. Now that I have managed to think more creatively, I have a better chance of capturing my readers' attention."

Ultimately, the way to keep the flow of useful questions going throughout the writing process is to think of yourself not only as a writer, but also as an editor. You may not be up to that job yet, but down the line you will see that editing is integral to the writing process. Of course, it would be great if we all had crackerjack editors at our disposal who could locate our flaws and correct them for us. For most of us, however, that is beyond any kind of practical reach.

Therefore, an enormous part of writing is learning how to be your own editor — that is, learning to self-edit. To self-edit, you must be able to ask yourself pertinent and probing questions every step of the way. For instance, "Are *pertinent* and *probing* the very best words I can use in this situation? Is *pertinent* a better word choice than *relevant?* Is it better than *germane?* Better than *apt?* What are the connotations connected to those words? Why is one better than the other?"

That kind of questioning might not be familiar to you, and you might regard it as overthinking. After all, isn't that sweating the small stuff? In fact, all that small stuff adds up to the overall impression you are leaving on your readers. In other words, every word counts.

My college applicants, especially the STEM majors, who represent the majority of my students, are fascinated by the degree of attention that we pay to a piece of writing. Now, you have to understand that these STEM folks are more than willing to devote scrupulous attention to their engineering projects, coding projects, or the many other efforts that fall within their bandwidth. The experience of devoting that kind of attention to writing — a pursuit that has essentially been outside of their interests for most of their lives — is revelatory. In very little time, as I work with them, they are right there with me, questioning every word and giving a piece of writing the full attention and respect it warrants.

Once you have gone through this process of asking yourself pointed questions, you might then want to formulate a short, creative brief. It can be as short as a few sentences and might sound something like this:

> My goal is to write a 750-word service piece, geared to a lay audience, in which the merits of composting are clearly laid out. I will assume that my reader has no prior knowledge of this subject. Following a general introduction on why composting is desirable for both the planet and the individual, I will make use of a series of subheads tied to specific steps in the composting process, such as Shredding and Chopping, Mixing Browns and Greens, Keeping It Watered, Keeping It Moving, and so on.

You get the idea. Now you can better understand your mission and proceed with some sense of clarity and purpose. Sure, things could change as the piece evolves, but for getting off square one such a creative brief can make a real difference.

## Getting Unstuck

Getting started and getting unstuck are two separate issues. Impediments like resistance and procrastination almost always precede the act of writing, and, to recap, we can attempt to deal with those through certain specific measures like setting a quota for the day, establishing a deadline, and asking ourselves questions to get the juices going. Then, however, we can be faced with the issue of getting stuck with the writing itself, which can happen even after we have moved past our dilatory behaviors.

Now is a good time to go back to Step One and reconsider the central question we discussed: "Who am I writing this for?" If the answer is "myself" (as with a journal entry, for instance), your writing experience is going to be very different from the one you will have if your answer is "my history professor." And who your history professor is — how smart and exacting and demanding she is — will also be important. Keeping your audience in mind, however, should help motivate you when you are stuck. Writing to a void is tough. Writing to a reader? Less so.

You might also attempt to get unstuck by jumping into some research. And by research, I don't mean getting lost on the internet. I think we've already addressed that issue. Rather, I am talking about research as an invigorating force that can enliven virtually any act of writing. Let's not forget that writing and learning are deeply symbiotic. When you write, you are putting yourself into a learning mode. You are expanding your thinking and probing your consciousness.

Keeping that in mind can be helpful even with those writing assignments that feel minor, and extending that learning mode to include some research can help unglue you when you are clearly stuck.

Let's imagine, for instance, that you are writing a letter to the manufacturer of your washing machine, whose repair history has been deeply disappointing to you. You're angry, you're having difficulty ordering your thinking about it, and you're sitting at your computer, feeling stuck. In this situation, you'll want to ask questions. What are you looking for? What kind of result are you hoping to get from this letter? What are you asking for? What are the impediments to getting what you are asking for? (Perhaps your washer is four years old, you haven't serviced it on an established schedule, and you attempted to wash a Turkish rug in it.) How are you going to address those impediments?

Feeling more focused (but still somewhat stuck), you might well turn to research. What is the repair record of your washing machine compared to those of machines made by other manufacturers? Are there other people on the internet complaining about Best-Ever washing machines? Yes, you are being drawn down that rabbit hole to some degree, but this time with a purpose. Hopefully, your research will invigorate the learning that is part of writing, and you will come away with some nuggets that can shape your letter in new and valuable ways.

That move toward research can work for you in many different writing situations, but if you continue to feel stuck, you may want to try a strategy called freewriting.

## Freewriting

One reason many of us have problems with writing is because we were taught in a way that focused largely on rules. Imagine learning to dance with a teacher who is primarily driving home all the things you are doing wrong — "Hip out! Leg in! Head up!" — instead of giving you a chance to experience the joy of movement and expression.

Well, guess what? There is the potential for considerable joy to be experienced in writing as well. Whenever we pursue creative expression and aesthetic excellence, we stand a chance of experiencing joy. The specter of that teacher who hectored us about rules continues to haunt many of us, however. We were told *never* to start a sentence with a conjunction and *never* to end a sentence with a preposition. We will debunk some of those rules later in this book, but for now let's just agree that too many rules inhibit writing. Freewriting allows you to step away from those rules and can be helpful in guiding you toward an easier relationship with the written word.

What exactly is freewriting? In short, it is writing *without rules*. When we freewrite, rules and regulations fall by the wayside. We simply set aside a prescribed amount of time — ten minutes is a good chunk — and we write, flying in the face of those rules. We do not care about punctuation, capitalization, verb-tense agreement, spelling, word usage, sentence structure, or any of those other issues that make the amateur (and sometimes even the professional) clench in fear. There does not have to be any set subject or any set goal. If you want to move from the merits of chardonnay to the mating habits of wombats to the word *vinegar* spelled out thirty times, it's all good. There are no judgments to be made and no results that need to be assessed. It is what it is.

This is not to say that there is nothing to be gleaned from freewriting beyond the limbering exercise that it is. In fact, you might have come up with a word or an image that you want to hold on to or that will inspire you to go in a certain direction. If you do, that's nice. If you don't, no harm. You aren't freewriting to achieve a result, after all. You are freewriting to get away from the tyranny of rules and to "free" yourself up for some actual writing.

Let's also note that you needn't restrict your freewriting only to the beginning of a writing session. If you get stuck in the middle of your piece and need to prime the pump again, go back into freewriting mode and see what happens. If nothing else, it will be a healthier distraction for you than playing poker online.

Let us also note that you may experience real resistance to freewriting at the start. After all, rules can be very powerful, often affecting us in wholly unconscious ways. On those occasions when I have asked a group to engage in freewriting, inevitably a few people appear to be visibly discomfited by the idea. They are suspicious of such freedom and may react by writing "This is stupid" over and over again. And they are doubly shocked when I tell them that it's perfectly okay for them to do that. In fact, maybe their response is an expression of their deep-seated feeling that writing is, in fact, stupid, because they were made to feel stupid early on in their writing experience. No one should ever feel that way — and freewriting is a great antidote to the tyranny of rules that have too long been imposed.

## P.S. Try This

Still stuck, eh? It happens. An emergency measure that can help when you're in that situation is to write your piece as a letter or an email to a friend. It's a trick of the mind that can work, as "rules" are once again put aside, and in their place is the friendly face of the person you are writing to. So even if you're wrestling with your letter about the faulty washing machine and even if you know in your head that your friend Anita is not going to be reading this, you may still have an easier time with the whole thing if you write it to Anita. It will feel more immediate, more connected, and you will feel less inhibited. The conversational quality of the "letter" will oil the machinery, and the words will be more likely to flow.

## Brainstorming

Even though I'm an avid believer in freewriting, it is only one strategy for getting a piece of writing underway. Brainstorming is another way to stimulate and collect your thoughts. Good thoughts are easily lost, and if you don't write them down, chances are they will fly away. Most of us are familiar with the practice of brainstorming, which is applicable to just about any situation in which focused thinking is required, from engineering to community organizing to debating to… writing, of course.

Brainstorming about a writing assignment can help you locate a topic, build an argument, develop a better understanding of what your topic is actually about, and more. It requires no special equipment and is entirely free, and even though exchanging ideas with others is perhaps the optimal form of brainstorming, it can also be done very well on your own.

When it comes to brainstorming, the cardinal rule is: *don't judge as you go*. The idea is to amass raw material, and once you have done that, you can become the judge of what stays and what goes. Right now, you are focused on producing some output related to a piece of writing, so this is not the time to pull back.

One of the main maneuvers you can use in your brainstorming sessions is called *cubing*. Cubes, as you know, have six sides, and when you are cubing, you are looking at a topic or an idea from multiple points of view. When cubing, you'll want to examine your idea or topic in these six ways:

1.  **Describe it.** Let's imagine you are spreading your writing wings by writing a restaurant review for your local newspaper. The first "side" of your cubing efforts will be focused on description, which is probably where you are initially inclined to go anyway. Then, drawing on your memory (or, better yet, on the notes you took while dining), you do your best to recapture the experience. You recall the blond wood walls, the hanging plants, the baguette on the table along with the little dish of herb butter, and so on and so forth. Put in as much description as you care to, but keep in mind that description is only one side of your cube.

2.  **Compare it.** Now turn to another "side" of the cube and compare this restaurant with others you've been

to. If it's a Thai restaurant you're writing about, then don't compare it to a Middle Eastern one. That would be like comparing apples and oranges. Instead, compare it to other Thai or Asian restaurants that hold a place in your memory. (Remember, you are only taking notes at this stage. You're not actually writing text.)

3. **Associate it.** When exploring a third "side" of the cube, you will likely consider some of the intangibles from your experience at that restaurant — its ambience, for instance. Did it remind you of a night you once spent in Bangkok, walking along the Chao Phraya River? Was the décor somehow reminiscent of something you saw in the Leonardo DiCaprio movie *The Beach*, which was set in Thailand? Some of your associations will probably wind up on the cutting-room floor as you get deeper into the writing, but you never know where they might lead you. For now, remember that you are trying to amass material, and *don't judge*.

4. **Analyze it.** While spending time on the fourth "side" of the cube, you will systematically weigh the various aspects of the overall dining experience. Your categories might include service, taste, value, and such. Under those headings, briefly note your thoughts and impressions.

5. **Apply it.** On the fifth "side" of the cube, you will be synthesizing your thoughts and impressions. The restaurant had good food and attentive service, but

what are some of the bigger-picture issues? Is this a restaurant you would go to on a first date? For a business meeting? Would you take your out-of-town parents there? How are you going to "apply" your overall impression of this restaurant, comparing it with so many of your other experiences dining out?

6. **Argue for it.** Finally, you'll bring together all your thinking and jot down points, both pro and con, regarding this particular restaurant. It was hot. It was cold. It was stuffy. The tables were too close together. The acoustics were bad. The bathroom was barely big enough to move around in. The headwaiter's cologne permeated the air. The food came late, and when it arrived, it was tepid and bland. Before you know it, your brainstorming will have left you filled with ideas and observations that will serve you well when you sit down to write.

Another form of brainstorming that many people rely on is *mapping*. Some people also refer to mapping as *clustering* or *webbing*, but whatever label you use, it is essentially a graphic approach to brainstorming. Here, the subject of your restaurant review — let's call it Buddha's Dream — sits in the middle of a graphic field. Branching off from that hub are a variety of topics, like menu, service, wine and beer, noise level, décor, parking, ease of reservations, and so on. You can have as many or as few branches as you wish — and your branches can have subbranches (service, for instance, might branch off to headwaiter, waiter, busboy, or what have you).

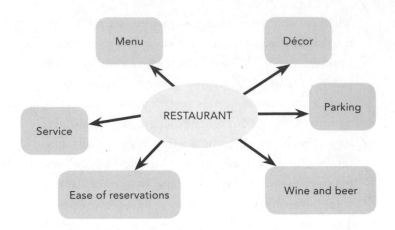

You needn't be a graphic artist or have any kind of artistic aptitude to successfully use mapping as a brainstorming technique. By the same token, mapping is a particularly useful tool for those who are visual-spatial learners rather than verbal-linguistic learners.

## Journaling

One of the best ways to organize your thinking about your writing is to keep a journal. Think of it as brainstorming on a long-range, ongoing basis. Of course, not everyone has the appetite for such a pursuit — but if you do, you're likely to benefit from it. Jack London, author of *The Call of the Wild*, *White Fang*, and other classics, had this advice to offer: "Keep a notebook. Travel with it, sleep with it. Slap into it every stray thought that flutters up into your brain. Cheap paper is less perishable than gray matter, and lead pencil markings endure longer than memory."

At times when I have advised people to keep a journal, some have resisted, protesting that such an activity was too "writerly" for them. I can understand that response. At first glance, there does seem something perhaps overly self-conscious about recording your thoughts and impressions in a little notebook you carry around. However, many people who have adopted the habit of journaling report that they have gained a great deal of insight into themselves and into writing as a result.

For some, journaling becomes a lifelong habit. For others, it is simply a phase. In either case, it can be very useful. What are some of the benefits of journaling? These come to mind:

- A journal is a good, central place in which to collect your thoughts.
- Journaling helps keep ideas from getting lost.
- Journaling encourages writing fluency. (The more you write, as encouraged by the daily habit of journaling, the more comfortable you get with it.)
- A journal is a safe writing zone, as no one who is uninvited gets to see your words, and no judgment is brought to bear on your writing.
- Journaling encourages a higher level of brainstorming. You can use your journal to store all your ideas. Embellish them to your heart's content in your journal — and then, if you choose, pull the plug on them. No one will know but you.

## Setting Up Your Scaffold

Hopefully, by now you are learning to handle the mind game that accompanies writing and have tamped down the fear, anxiety, and procrastination that seem to afflict all who put pen to paper (or fingers to keyboard). Perhaps you have set a daily quota for yourself, and that has helped a bit. Perhaps you have imposed a deadline, arbitrary or real. Have you asked yourself those very important questions that are meant to bring to light some valuable thinking? Perhaps you've also done a bit of research to further your thinking. Very likely, you have engaged in some freewriting to limber up your writing muscles, and let us also assume that you have made time for brainstorming or mapping.

Altogether, things are feeling somewhat calmer, so now you're ready to move ahead with more intention, concentration, and commitment. A good next step would be to set up a scaffold, for this is the point in the writing process when you will begin to feel the need for the security of structure. The best and most proven way to get that sense of security is to create an outline of some sort.

I say "of some sort," because, to tell the truth, I have not always been the most assiduous outliner. In fact, I have written entire novels without ever sitting down to do an outline. In retrospect, maybe that wasn't the best method (even though most of my novels were published), but I did it for two reasons: (1) I am a confident writer and know that if I don't wind up where I thought I would, I can always make adjustments, and (2) when writing fiction, I have always enjoyed the feeling of working without a net and not knowing where I might land.

You, however, might not have that kind of confidence in your writing. If that is the case, then you will want to set yourself up with an outline or some outline-like schematic before you get down to the actual writing.

I say "outline-like schematic," because you needn't feel that you must create a traditional, standard outline for your piece, with the usual Roman and Arabic numbers, capped and lowercased letters, and the proper indents. Of course, if you want to do that, then by all means go right ahead. Surely, you learned in school how that kind of outline works. But in the interest of not bringing more rules to bear on this thing we call writing, be aware that writers generally wind up devising strategies that work for them — or at least that work for the piece of writing they are undertaking. So when I say "outline" or "scaffold," I am talking about a tool that will allow you to move forward with your work.

Think of that restaurant review again (although this time let's go French instead of Thai). The outline/scaffold for that piece could be a very simple thing, something that looks like this:

I will start with the high point of my meal at Le Bicycle (the succulent braised lamb shank with polenta, mushrooms, and escarole). I will try to recapture the delight of that moment, but then, regretfully, I will need to discuss some of the negatives:

The blue-point oyster appetizer arrived lukewarm.

The Caesar salad was slightly wet.

The dessert menu was unimaginative.

The wine list was overpriced.

Next I'll give a nod to the pleasing décor — the
bicycle motif, carried out with actual mounted bikes,
some of them antique, as well as graphic images of all
kinds of bikes decorating the walls. But restaurants are
really about the food, aren't they? I will conclude with
a nod to the capable service and then an expression of
hope that Le Bicycle's kitchen will rise in the future to
the level of that delicious lamb.

Something as brief and pointed as the above might be all
you need to stay focused on your writing. If at any point you
begin to feel lost (and most likely you will), you can ask questions that are meant to lend clarity to your purpose:

- What do I want to say?
- What structure allows me to best say it?
- What kind of examples do I need to support what I
  am saying?
- How do I end?
- What do I want my readers to know, understand, or
  feel by the time they get to the end of my piece?

With these thoughts in mind, you should be able to move
ahead with your writing.


## Up Close

For this lesson, I thought it would be interesting to share a
piece of my own that I wrote a few years ago when I published a book called *Having the Last Say: Capturing Your Legacy in One Small Story*. That book encourages older writers

to uncover a story that exemplifies an ethical value by which they have lived and then develop it into a 500- to 1,000-word narrative that can be shared as a keepsake with friends and family or even be read at their memorial service. In promoting interest in the book, I wrote a number of short pieces that I hoped would be placed in magazines and online. The one below was featured on the *Daily Beast* and concerns the power of storytelling. Have a look, and then I will discuss how I handled some of the writing issues that came up for me.

## THE LIFESAVING POWER OF STORYTELLING
## (*DAILY BEAST*, SEPTEMBER 24, 2015)

In many ways, my father was not an easy man. Something of a martinet, he lived with a huge amount of anxiety that he freely displaced onto others and, while he was enormously smart, his view of the world was, in certain respects, quite circumscribed. A true child of the Depression, he grew up behind his parents' dress shop in the Bronx and turned to popular cultural icons of the time like Horatio Alger and Dink Stover to figure out how to navigate the world. He lived to be 91 years old, mostly with some real quality of life, and when he died, I eulogized him. Trying to figure out what aspects felt right to pick out of our complicated 60-year relationship, I focused on how he had given me a love for stories.

Dad was a CPA who ultimately came to regard the reading of novels as frivolous, but he was, nonetheless, a wonderful natural storyteller. Throughout

my childhood, our moments of greatest intimacy came
when he told me bedtime stories. Sometimes he read
other people's stories to us. (I can still recall the grisly
accounts from Herbert Asbury's *The Gangs of New
York* of acid baths and bitten-off ears preserved in jars.)
Better yet were the stories from his childhood. There
was one I particularly loved about a race riot in which
he had become embroiled that featured narrow escapes
worthy of Indiana Jones. While none of these stories
would have been granted the parenting seal of approval,
they surely fueled my interest in fiction.

Emulating my father in this respect, I always made
a point of telling stories to my two sons, and now my
older son tells stories to his children. In this way, we
are passing along family history, cultural values, and
ethical guidelines for how we think life should be lived.
I wager that most people in the world have, on occa-
sion at least, tried to do the same with their offspring,
but this critical work too often gets lost in the shuffle
of today's overprogrammed childhoods. We must as-
cribe equal importance to the lessons in life that we gain
through stories as we do to the lessons that our children
learn on the cello, in tennis, and in coding.

Studies have confirmed the power and importance
of storytelling. In the mid-'90s, psychologist Marshall
Duke created the "Did You Know" scale to help explore myth and ritual in American families, asking children to answer a series of questions, such as "Do you
know where your parents met?" or "Do you know the
story of your birth?" Duke found that the more children knew about their family histories, the more sense

of control they had over their life, which, in turn, resulted in higher self-esteem.

I believe that most of us understand, at least intuitively, how important it is to tell stories to young children, in order to give them an understanding of their place in the continuum. Simply put, storytelling is cozy, constructive, and a win-win for parent and child alike. We forget, however, that the power of storytelling is available to us throughout our lives — and throughout the lives of our children.

Curling up with your adult child on a comfy Morris chair is obviously not an interest or an option for most people, and so if storytelling is to continue to be exchanged between parent and child, it almost inevitably will involve more formal constructs. To that end, many people today are engaging in memoir writing or are taping oral histories with the idea of leaving family stories behind. While I admire those who pursue such activities, many others fall by the wayside on account of the commitment and discipline that is required. I also recognize how difficult it is to craft a memoir that will sustain the interest of the reader — or the writer.

I have worked with adult, nonprofessional writers on stories of limited length — let's say, 500 to 1,000 words — and have found that their short narratives allow them to plumb the human condition with remarkable courage, candor, and often great skill. They write them for all the same reasons that anyone has ever written anything: to connect with other people; to come to terms with something in the past; to better understand something in physical or human nature; to pass along a tradition; to explore an ethical value or moral standard; to amuse; to confess; to forgive or be forgiven.

I have seen these writers create powerful stories about such things as joyfully singing in a choir even when struggling with chronic obstructive pulmonary disease brought on by years of smoking or coping with a wife's cancer by teaching dance to cancer survivors. And while these writers are no longer using stories to tuck their children into bed, some have reported that they transformed the Thanksgiving table with their reading of them.

In telling these stories, they are doing exactly what Atul Gawande talks about in his book *Being Mortal*. "As people become aware of the finitude of their life, they do not ask for much. They do not seek more riches. They do not seek more power," Gawande writes. "They ask only to be permitted, insofar as possible, to keep shaping the story of their life in the world."

Storytelling is as basic to the human experience as music, dance, or sports. In our busy world, we can't afford to leave it behind for it is too good for us and for our children. Storytelling can lend clarity and purpose to life's third act, when disorder and a lack of relevancy loom, and it can give clarity, purpose, and strength to those whom we will one day leave behind.

I quite like this piece and was glad that the *Daily Beast* decided to publish it. Was it complicated to write? Not particularly, for writing has become much less complicated for me after so many years of doing it. This is not to say that the emotional and psychological challenges that any writer faces do not beset me as well. I faced some of the same resistance when I sat down to write this piece as you do when you initially confront your writing assignments, and I indulged in the same kinds of procrastinating behaviors to avoid the work. Once I got past that, however, which I managed to do using my tried-and-true procrastination busters, I felt quickly at home because I had worked up my outline to guide me.

Before actually sitting down to write, I asked myself a series of questions like the ones we have been discussing throughout this step. This is what that dialogue with myself looked like:

- **What do I want to say?**
  I want to convey that storytelling is a force that has significant importance in human development.
- **What structure allows me to best say it?**
  I think the best way to start is to discuss the role of storytelling in my own personal development. I will relate the story of my father as storyteller, because my relationship with my father was laden with conflict and that will lend extra power to the piece.
- **What kind of examples do I need to support what I am saying?**
  In this piece, I will move from my personal experience with storytelling to some general information drawn from psychologists about the impact of storytelling on people's lives. I will then go to examples of how the writers in my book *Having the Last Say* used storytelling to gain insight into their lives and

how their stories have illuminated their lives for their
loved ones.

- **How do I end?**
  I will use an appropriate quote from an important recent book and then craft a final summary.

- **What do I want my readers to know, understand, or
  feel by the time they get to the end of my piece?**
  I want them to appreciate why storytelling is as important as it is — and I also want to motivate them to
  go buy my book.

Again, in writing this piece I faced all the other issues that
every writer faces: finding the right words, untangling clunky
syntax, enlivening flat prose, catching faulty grammar, and
all the rest. At this point in my writing career, however, those
technical issues don't scare me. I know I can handle them.
Rather, the structural issues I faced at the outset were the
challenge — and the source of the anxiety. Before long, however, having asked and answered my key questions, I had my
outline and was on my way.

One more thing: our next step is called "Tell Stories."
Keep my piece in mind, if you will, because we will be discussing the power that can be derived from storytelling.

## ROUNDUP

1. Fear and writing go hand in hand. Learn to live with
   that reality.
2. One response to fear is procrastination, which can be
   insidious.

3. Several strategies can combat procrastination, including setting quotas and deadlines for yourself.

4. Asking questions is a great way to jump-start a piece of writing.

5. Keeping your audience in mind helps you get unstuck, as does jumping into some research.

6. Freewriting is an inventive way of loosening up for a writing assignment.

7. When truly stuck, try writing your piece as a letter or an email to a friend.

8. Learn the art and science of brainstorming. It will help you immeasurably in your writing efforts.

9. Journaling is a fine habit for anyone who is interested in becoming a better writer.

10. Craft an outline or some other scaffold to guide your writing work.

# Tell Stories

Author Philip Pullman, creator of the bestselling fantasy trilogy His Dark Materials, has said, "After nourishment, shelter, and companionship, stories are the thing we need most in the world." Now, if you don't fancy yourself a reader, you may reflexively reject that premise. "I haven't read a novel in eight years!" you proudly declare. Well, perhaps so. But have you seen a movie? Watched a television show? Listened to a joke? Read *Goodnight Moon* to a child? Stayed up late with a nonfiction book that *read* like a story? Played *The Legend of Zelda*? I suspect so.

Since we humans live our lives along narrative lines — we are born, we work, some wed, some bear children, some suffer, some thrive, some prevail, we die — we are hardwired to respond to the narrative form. Narratives, or stories, help us understand life; they also serve to educate, entertain, preserve folkways and traditions, and instill moral and ethical values.

Anthropologists have uncovered narratives at the heart of every culture throughout the world, as human beings have made up stories and listened to them since the beginning of time. We humans look for the recognizable patterns of narratives in so many corners of our existence. We even look for them where they are not intended.

In the 1940s, the noted Austrian gestalt psychologist Fritz Heider collaborated with Marianne Simmel, whose research was in cognitive neuropsychology. Together they produced a landmark work known as "An Experimental Study of Apparent Behavior." The thirty-four participants in this study were shown a short animated film in which three geometric shapes — a large triangle, a smaller one, and a circle — moved at various speeds in various directions. The only other shape on the screen, a rectangle that was open on one side, remained stationary.

Out of the thirty-four participants, only one saw the film in a wholly literal way — as geometric shapes moving around the screen and nothing more. All the other participants brought their own life experience and points of reference to the film to create stories about these shapes. Some saw the triangles as two men fighting. Others interpreted the circle as a damsel in distress, fleeing the men's aggression. People conferred the human emotions of anger, fear, and jealousy on these nonhuman shapes. In essence, even back in the 1940s, they turned this short, simple film into a Pixar blockbuster.

So let's go back to what I was saying at the beginning of this step. Even though you might reflexively reject the position that stories are of vital human importance, in fact you are telling stories and hearing stories day in and day out. And if you allow yourself to draw on the great human tradition of storytelling, you will come to see how you can enliven your writing in a wide range of situations.

As a novelist and playwright, I have always been interested in the narrative form, but became particularly aware of its power when I began to work on admission essays with college applicants. I reasoned that the entire objective of the college-admission essay is to make oneself memorable. Unfortunately, too many people use that situation as an invitation to promote their achievements and accomplishments, generally in a flat and linear way. This produces what I refer to as the "résumé essay." Such an essay totally misses the real point of this assignment, which is to make yourself memorable by connecting emotionally with your reader.

I tell students to imagine themselves seated at a party next to someone they don't know. Would they try to connect by touting their achievements? ("Did you know that I'm the number-four nationally ranked tennis player in the eastern United States?" or "Are you aware that I received a perfect 800 score on my chemistry achievement test?") Inevitably, that sounds wrong to their ears, so I tell them to imagine themselves instead starting a conversation with a story. ("Guess what I saw today on the subway?" or "Did you hear about the dog that fell down a well on State Street?") Unless you're seated next to someone exceedingly aloof, chances are you're going to grab that person's attention — and even hold it — if you can tell your story well. (Like most things in life, there is a right way and a wrong way to tell a story, and I'm going to tell you the right way.)

Are you still feeling some resistance to this whole story

business? "When I bought a book about how to become a confident writer, I wasn't signing up to become a storyteller," I can almost hear you say. I think your resistance may begin to fade, however, as I show you how powerful even a bit of narrative flair can be when it comes to your writing challenges.

Again, going back to my college applicants, I think of the essays that many of them are asked to write about a favorite extracurricular activity. By the time we get around to that essay, we have already finished the personal statement, which is decidedly narrative in feeling, so all I have to say is, "Remember to tell a story." Let me give you a quick example of what I'm talking about.

I had a student who wanted to write his extracurricular essay about coaching soccer with young kids. The word limit on this essay was only 150 words, so that meant there wasn't much space to move around in. Still, I maintained that he could get a lot more out of that allotment than he made use of in his initial draft, which looked like this:

> Since my sophomore year in 2015, I have been working on a weekly basis with the North Shore Special Needs Sports Buddies Program. In this capacity, I help elementary-school kids feel better about themselves through the experience of sports. It is very gratifying to take my expertise at soccer and apply it to this situation, helping a young person feel better about himself or herself. This volunteer work has also helped me build up certain skills and abilities that will help me later in life. For instance, I have become a better communicator and I am more patient than I used to be. I have also come to see that the world is made up of all kinds of people

and that those with special needs can teach me things as well. I will hope to do more of this work in the future. ·

What do you think? Would that grab the attention of someone who didn't know this young man, someone who is forming an impression of him and deciding whether he should join their college community? Or does it simply sit there, not going anywhere, not saying much? The solution I recommended was to inject some narrative flair into the piece. Here is the revision, still at 150 words:

> "Keep your body over the ball, Max," I tell the fourth-grader in my charge, "and your head down."
>
> Every Sunday for the last two years, I have worked as a counselor at the North Shore Special Needs Sports Buddies Program in Swampscott, Massachusetts, with elementary-school kids like Max. My goal is to introduce these boys and girls, who have a range of physical problems and developmental delays, to the joy of sports. They have learned a lot about concentration and determination from our sessions and have taught me about those things as well. My patience and my ability to communicate have become much stronger as a result of our connection — but the smiles I see on their faces are the real bonus.
>
> "Okay, Max," I say, patting his back and sending him onto the field. "Give it your all."
>
> I watch as he races about. It is something to see.

Now do you have a sense of what I mean when I talk about narrative flair? Don't you feel that you know this person better? Don't you *want* to know this person better? And eliciting the kind of connection and communication that results from such storytelling can be applied to countless writing and public-speaking situations.

Think about it. What is the tone of this book that you're reading right now? Am I telling you dry facts, or am I sharing a kind of story with you? If it feels more like the latter, how am I managing to do that? After all, there are no dragons or cowboys or Roman centurions in this story. How am I capturing your interest (if indeed I am)? I suspect I am doing so by using a storytelling tone that brings you into my circle, right by the fire where it's nice and warm and where I can give you things to think about.

Storytelling is a natural gift that some lucky people possess. If you think of all the people you know, surely you will recognize that some are good at telling stories and some are not. But the narrative is also a form that can be learned, the way a dance move or a golf swing can be learned. Even if you do not think of yourself as a natural storyteller, you can still become much better at working with narratives, and eventually you will be able to call upon that skill to enliven your writing whenever you wish. So let's start thinking about this narrative form and how it works.

## Tell Me a Story

Chances are, you can remember saying, "Tell me a story," to your mother or father or a grandparent. Whichever storyteller you turned to, you had certain expectations about what you were looking to receive. And if you didn't receive it, you were disappointed.

Even at a very young age, you probably had a sense of what made for a good story and what didn't — and you probably had a sense of who the good storytellers were in your life. They were the people who intuitively understood the form of the narrative, and even though you didn't know the elements of that form, you could still sense when the form was well executed and when it flopped.

Let's tell a story right now, shall we?

Jacob was seated on the Long Island Railroad, heading into Manhattan from Valley Stream, where he was living back home with his family following his graduation from college. He had been there for six long months, going for job interviews and coming away empty-handed. Today, he was on his way to an interview with Cisco, hoping to get an entry-level job in coding. Coding was his passion, and he desperately wanted to get his life started. He didn't want to live in his parents' home because, as cool as they were about it, it made him feel like a child.

When he got off at Penn Station, he walked up to Broadway and hopped on a bus. It was packed, and he had to stand for a while before a seat opened up. When he sat down, he looked over the list of anticipated interview questions he had put together. He had googled "Microsoft interviews" and prepared himself for some possible brain crunchers like, "Design an ATM for children" or "What is your favorite software and how would you improve it?" As he tried to concentrate, his palms got sweaty. He had better not blow this opportunity.

The bus stopped, more people got on, and suddenly

he became aware of an elderly woman standing in front of him. With covert glances, he could see that she was well dressed and stood tall enough, with no cane or anything, but still she looked as though she was maybe eighty. Should he get up and give her his seat? His mom always told him he should open doors for people, say "please" and "thank you," and offer his seat to pregnant women and the elderly. She said it was the mark of a gentleman.

Looking around, however, he didn't see any other men jumping up to do the right thing. He tried to stay focused on his questions, looking down at his pad, but the woman was standing right in front of him, carrying a giant pocketbook, and it was a warm July day.

He couldn't resist any longer. "Excuse me, Ma'am. Would you like to sit down?"

She looked at him for a moment, in surprise, and then sneered, "What do I look like? Some old wreck?"

With a big *harrumph*, she turned around and grabbed a strap on the other side of the bus.

People on either side of him looked away, in a kind of embarrassment, as he shrunk in his seat. He felt deeply stung — at the exact moment when he didn't need that kind of distraction.

Soon the bus came to his stop, and he got off. As he walked along Fourteenth Street, he felt people's eyes on him. All the confidence he tried to muster was gone. How could he have been so stupid and inappropriate with that woman? And then, just as he was berating himself, two young Asian girls stopped him.

In very halting English, they asked him if he knew

how to get to Times Square. In fact, although he didn't know the city all that well, he knew the answer to that question and pointed out the direction in which they should head. They smiled and thanked him many times, and as they walked off, he realized that he felt better. He realized too that he mustn't let anyone else's behavior determine his self-worth. He didn't know what that woman's problem was — but he didn't have a problem. He was a good person who liked to help people, and what's wrong with that?

With a lighter step, he moved toward his destination, feeling convinced that this time he was going to shine.

Now, if you had asked someone to tell you a story and this is what that person came up with, how would you feel about it? Well, perhaps it's not the greatest story you ever heard — but, in fact, I deliberately chose a story that wasn't going to be the greatest story you ever heard. I was just looking for a regular old story, such as anyone might share, that would still have the four critical elements of a story, so that you would feel (presumably) that your narrative hunger had been addressed.

Before I get to those four elements and demonstrate how this story uses them, let me give you another draft of the story, so that I can refer to it as well:

Jacob boarded the bus on his way from Penn Station to Fourteenth Street in Manhattan. Today, he had an interview with Cisco for an entry-level job in coding. Since graduating from college six months ago, he had been going for job interviews but coming away empty-handed. Today, he had one more chance, and he really wanted this job. Coding was his passion, and he desperately wanted to get his life started. He didn't want to live in his parents' home anymore because, as cool as they were about it, it made him feel like a child.

The bus was packed, and he had to stand. Finally, he got a seat, which gave him the opportunity to look over the list of anticipated interview questions he had put together. As he tried to concentrate, his palms got sweaty. He hoped he wouldn't blow this opportunity too.

The bus stopped, more people got on, and suddenly he became aware of an elderly woman standing in front of him. With covert glances, he could see that she was well dressed and stood tall enough, with no cane or anything, but still she looked as though she was maybe eighty. Should he get up and give her his seat? His mom always told him he should open doors for people, say "please" and "thank you," and offer his seat to pregnant women and the elderly.

Looking around, however, he didn't see any other men jumping up to do the right thing. He tried to stay focused on his questions, but the woman was standing right in front of him, carrying a giant pocketbook, and it was a warm July day.

He couldn't resist any longer. "Excuse me, Ma'am. Would you like to sit down?"

She looked at him in surprise and then sneered, "What do I look like? Some old wreck?"

With a big *harrumph*, she turned around and grabbed a strap on the other side of the bus.

He felt deeply stung — at exactly the moment when he didn't need that kind of distraction.

When the bus came to his stop, he got off and walked along Fourteenth Street, feeling everyone's eyes on him. All the confidence he tried to muster was gone. How could he have been so stupid and inappropriate with that woman?

And then, just as he was berating himself, two young Asian girls stopped him. In very halting English, they asked him if he knew how to get to Times Square. He pointed the way, and they smiled and thanked him many times. As they walked off, he realized that he felt better. He realized too that he mustn't let anyone else's behavior determine his self-worth. He didn't know what that woman's problem was — but he didn't have a problem. He was a good person who liked to help people, and what's wrong with that?

With a lighter step, he moved toward his destination, convinced that this time he was going to shine.

Let's look at what happened between those two versions. The big change is that I found 117 words to take out. Do you remember the section back in Step One when we talked about the contract between writer and reader in which the writer promises to deliver a piece of writing that is concise?

I immediately saw that I could honor the "conciseness" clause of the writer-reader contract by lopping off significant chunks of text right at the beginning. Was there any reason to start the story on the Long Island Railroad? Not a bit. It was an easy cut and served the purpose of bringing more unity and cohesion (i.e., fewer places to get to and from) to the story. We will think about this issue again momentarily, when we talk about The Once, the first of the four elements of a narrative that storytellers must grapple with.

All other cuts were of the kind that I call "invisible." Words here, words there. Nothing any reader — or writer — ever misses. If you have the time, play the game by comparing the two pieces and see if you can figure out what I cut.

Again, I'm assuming you found this to be a reasonably good story, in the sense that it held your attention. If that's the case, let's figure out how this story functioned.

## The Elements of the Narrative

A moment ago, I told you that the narrative is a form that can be learned, like a dance move or a golf swing. Take the latter, for instance. *Golfweek* breaks down the form of the golf swing into four components: grip, setup, takeaway and backswing, and follow-through. Similarly, we're going to break down the narrative into four elements: The Once, The Ordinary vs. the Extraordinary, Conflict and Tension, and The Point. When you understand how these elements act and interact, you'll have a much stronger sense of how to tell a story.

### The Once

One of the first problems a writer must figure out when undertaking a narrative is how to handle time. After all, no writer (or reader) has all the time in the world. Every single narrative ever told, from a knock-knock joke to *Gone with the Wind*, has had to deal with that issue. Those that have survived have dealt with it successfully.

The Once is that specific point in time at which your narrative is set — and narratives always have a beginning point. Think of fairy tales and "Once upon a time." Think of the Bible and "In the beginning." Think of *Moby Dick* and "Call me Ishmael." Think of *The Color Purple* and "You better not tell nobody but God." The beginning of any piece of writing is usually the most difficult part. You need to set a mood and a tone that will invite your reader in, and that is a challenge.

As with so much of writing, the work involves a good deal of trial and error. If your first opening doesn't work, just bag it and go on to the next one. You've seen that movie where the frustrated writer keeps pulling sheets of paper from the typewriter, crumpling them up, and throwing them in the overflowing wastebasket? (We're talking about period movies here; very few writers crumple papers anymore.) That's a visual representation of the trial-and-error process I am describing.

Sometimes all you need to break through the challenge of The Once is some serious pruning at the start of your piece. Maybe all you have to do, in fact, is lop off a chunk. Take the example of the story I just shared about the young man on the bus on his way to a job interview. If you recall, in the initial draft, the action began on the train to the city. By the time we got to the second draft, the train had been lopped off and the story started right on the bus. Result? A much tighter story and a far defter handling of The Once.

I see this kind of problem and resolution all the time

with my college applicants. They'll decide to write a narrative about their two-week trip to Louisiana to build houses with Habitat for Humanity, let's say, and they'll start in their room, back in New Hampshire, as they're packing their bags. Or they'll start on the plane to New Orleans. Or they'll start on the tarmac at the Louis Armstrong New Orleans International Airport. By the time we finish our work, all those openings have gone away.

Sometimes we have to be very patient until we get The Once just right. The reason for that is because it is not unusual for writers to not really know or understand what a piece is about until they are well into it. "Ah! Now I see that this piece is not just about baseball; it's really about my relationship with my father!" And then, when that understanding clicks in, a writer can go back and readjust the time accordingly. The parts of the narrative that don't work toward the real theme of the piece can be pruned back or discarded altogether, leaving more room to support the theme that has now been identified. (And when I say "room," that applies to works of all length. Whether you have 100 words or 100,000 words to work with, the implicit contract between writer and reader remains the same, and part of that contract is focused on not wasting your reader's time.)

The college applicant who is writing about building houses in Louisiana cannot expect a reader to be satisfied with a flabby travelogue. That writer must locate the *meaning* of her story. Is it about being thrown in with people she might never have met otherwise? Is it about overcoming a feeling of ineptitude that has accompanied her all her life? Is it about escaping her overprotective family and experiencing the exhilaration of being on her own? Any or all of those could be worthy themes to explore, but once the writer decides which of those is the real story she wants to tell, then she can begin to tailor the time to support that story. As I say, writers need to be patient, because often that kind of insight does not emerge until the drafting process is well underway.

## The Ordinary vs. the Extraordinary

Another essential challenge that a writer faces when constructing a narrative is to figure out the "extraordinary" thing in the story that is going to arrest the reader's attention. Let's go back to the young man on the bus again. If that young man, Jacob, just sat on the bus, reviewed his interview questions, got off the bus, and entered the building where the interview was taking place, there would be no story. Instead, something extraordinary has to happen, that is, something *out of the ordinary*. That moment occurs when Jacob offers the elderly woman his seat and she becomes highly annoyed with him. Now, if he had offered the elderly woman his seat and she took it with a thank-you, that would have been somewhat out of the ordinary — after all, it's not every day that you get to be so gallant — but it's not quite out of the ordinary enough to arrest a reader's attention.

Keep in mind that all sorts of options are available for fulfilling the ordinary-vs.-extraordinary mandate for this bus story. Let's imagine, for instance, that the elderly woman boards the bus — and then collapses. Our hero, Jacob, springs into action, administering the CPR he learned in a first-responders course until medical personnel arrive on the scene.

As he watches the woman being loaded onto the stretcher, he realizes that his actions have cost him that coveted job, as the time for the interview has come and gone, but he also understands that he chose the more important course of action and feels okay about himself.

Or what if a very pretty girl sits down across from Jacob and starts to flirt with him? He flirts back, time passes, and before he knows it, he is two stops past his and late for the interview, which means he will not be getting that job. That's sufficiently out of the ordinary (it's not every day, after all, that a pretty girl flirts with you), but this particular action sends the story in a more comic direction (well, tragicomic perhaps, as he badly needed that job).

Your story is your story. You choose. But whatever choice you make, you must locate the extraordinary thing that either ignites or "turns" your story. In other words, the extraordinary thing does not have to take place at the beginning of the story, but could occur farther along in the narrative. Think again of the story of Jacob on the bus. Think about how the elderly woman's reaction to his kind offer, which occurred substantially into the story, "turned" the narrative and made it go in a more dramatic and ultimately meaningful direction. That is what you are looking for in a story, and without it you won't have a story.

## Conflict and Tension

The "extraordinary" event that ignites or turns the narrative does not take place in a vacuum. It needs to be connected to a second frame that shapes your narrative, and that frame has to do with conflict and tension. Let's look at this another way. The Once — where in time your narrative is situated — is one kind of frame (a time frame), and superimposed on top of that frame is another frame that has to do with conflict and tension. Although offering your seat to an elderly woman on a bus and having her throw the gesture back in your face is certainly an extraordinary event, it does not stand by itself. It exists (or at least should exist) in a framework of conflict and tension.

In Jacob's case, this unsettling incident ultimately helped him resolve feelings of insecurity about himself that might have affected his performance at a job interview. So the tension for Jacob was about his current life situation, in which he had recently graduated from college, was living at home with his parents, had no job, and was unsure of his prospects. The heart of the conflict in the story emerges when the elderly woman, in a surprising turn of events, rejects Jacob's kind offer in an extremely hostile way. At first, this rejection intensifies the tension for Jacob, making him feel worse about himself. Why was he such an idiot? Why so inappropriate? (And, implicitly, how will he ever get a job if that's who he is?) But then his altogether different and more positive interaction with the two young Asian tourists "turns" the narrative once again and leads to a positive resolution of his conflict. He *is* a good person, after all, he thinks, as he strides toward his interview with a new sense of confidence.

It is important to understand that if Jacob's conflict was of a different nature, then the extraordinary event would have been different. For instance, Jacob's conflict might be that he is passive and has not been pursuing a job with any kind of real intention. He is just as passive about noticing the elderly woman standing in front of him and thinking to offer her his seat. She must finally say to him, "Excuse me, young man, but this is a hot day, and I'm an old woman." Having someone say that to you would, in fact, be an extraordinary event. It would also send the narrative off in a very different direction to resolve the conflict and tension. (He gets up, thanks her for her straightforwardness, and realizes it is time to grow up.)

Keep in mind too that the main reason we all read, go to a movie, watch TV, or even play video games is to see how our heroes resolve conflict. Whether that hero is Hamlet or Arya Stark from *Game of Thrones*, we want to see how people (or characters) resolve conflict, that is, how they *live*, as life is essentially about conflict and how we resolve it.

Simply put, conflict is the struggle between opposing forces. Conflicts can occur between individuals (Superman and Lex Luthor), between groups (the Montagues and the Capulets in *Romeo and Juliet*), between individuals and society (Josef K. and the totalitarian bureaucracy in Franz Kafka's *The Trial*), between individuals and their own self-destruction (the unnamed insomniac hero of Chuck Palahniuk's *Fight Club*), between individuals and nature (Daniel Defoe's *Robinson Crusoe*), and more. Conflict can be immediately identifiable, as when Little Red Riding Hood comes up against the Big Bad Wolf in the fairy tale, or it can be subtle and even difficult to figure out, as in the driving force behind Don Draper's mysterious and destructive course in the TV series *Mad Men*. Whenever you tell a story, it is imperative that you have some aspect of conflict in it (otherwise, why tell it?), and when you examine it, the conflict will likely fall within one of the categories just cited.

## The Point

The last of the four elements that will play a critical role in your narrative is The Point. By the end of any given narrative, readers should come away with an understanding of why they have been asked to read it. They should have a sense of having come away with something real, whether it is an insight or a feeling, a laugh or a cry, a sense of indignation or empathy, or any number of other reactions. They should know The Point of what they have read.

Sometimes The Point of a narrative jumps out and shakes you by the hand. Take the fables of Aesop, with which you are probably familiar. Consider, if you will, "The Milkmaid and Her Pail." The young woman is going to market with a pail of milk on her head, fantasizing about all the things she'll buy when she cashes her milk in for coin. When she gives her head an impetuous toss, the pail falls to the ground, the milk is spilled, and her fantasies are dashed. The Point of the story is clearly stated in a moral (present in every Aesop fable): "Don't count your chickens until they're hatched."

Although you may choose to explicitly state The Point in your narrative, there is absolutely no obligation to do so, and modern readers may prefer to have The Point brought home with more subtlety. Turn again to the case of our young hero, Jacob, on the bus. What is The Point of that story? To a certain degree, that depends on what the reader brings to it — and readers naturally bring all kinds of preconceptions, biases, and other external forces to bear on a piece of writing.

For some readers the takeaway is: "Never give your seat to anyone on a bus (and be especially wary of elderly ladies)." Others may conclude: "Of course he was rejected. Giving up your seat for a woman, however old, is outmoded gender-normative behavior." And some will read it in sync with the writer's goal here, which is to have us recognize that other people's perceptions of us are not nearly as important as our perception of ourselves.

Again, please note that The Point does not ever have to be made explicit. It can be very subtle and require that readers devote significant thought to drawing it out. There is nothing wrong with that. Writing is a two-way street, and making readers do their part of the job is completely appropriate and often quite welcome.

## The Power of Storytelling

Now that you have a sense of how a narrative is constructed and understand the four critical elements that distinguish all narratives, or stories, let's think again about the storyteller's power to enliven different kinds of writing assignments.

Earlier in this chapter, I gave you the example of how one of my students was able to enliven a college-admission essay about an extracurricular activity with some narrative flair. He introduced Max, one of the kids he was coaching in a special-needs sports program, and created some action (i.e., time-specific coaching instruction) that felt narrative in nature. If you compare the first and second versions of the essay, you can see that the writer transformed his piece into a story. Not an epic, edge-of-your-seat story, but a small vignette that still manages to satisfy the reader's hardwired human interest in the narrative. And, interestingly, if you examine that story, you will see that the four elements of the narrative are in place. It's short, so let me bring it back for a second look:

"Keep your body over the ball, Max," I tell the fourth-grader in my charge, "and your head down."

Every Sunday for the last two years, I have worked as a counselor at the North Shore Special Needs Sports Buddies Program in Swampscott, Massachusetts, with elementary-school kids like Max. My goal is to introduce these boys and girls, who have a range of physical problems and developmental delays, to the joy of sports. They have learned a lot about concentration and determination from our sessions and have taught me about those things as well. My patience and my ability to communicate have become much stronger as a result of our connection — but the smiles I see on their faces are the real bonus.

"Okay, Max," I say, patting his back and sending him onto the field. "Give it your all."

I watch as he races about. It is something to see.

First, the writer deftly deals with the element of The Once. He decided to use a very tight close-up on the activity and so began with an *in media res* ("in the middle of things") opening. In other words, he jumps right into the action, with no words wasted.

The Ordinary vs. the Extraordinary is the element that

seems least present. That's because the moment is a small and quiet one. That's okay, however, given the tight space here. There's little opportunity in a piece of 150 words to tell a big story with a big extraordinary event. So, then, the extraordinary event of this narrative lies in the telling of it. That is to say, the writer is pulling a quiet, small, and potentially unnoticed moment out of a broader experience and, by examining it closely, turning it into an "extraordinary" moment (or event).

The Conflict and Tension frame can certainly be seen in this section:

> They have learned a lot about concentration and determination from our sessions and have taught me about those things as well. My patience and my ability to communicate have become much stronger as a result of our connection — but the smiles I see on their faces are the real bonus.

We feel the conflict and tension in the fact that the writer suggests — that is, lets us know, though not through any explicit statement — that his patience and communication may have been somewhat lacking. When the writer tells us that he has indeed learned much from these children, the conflict and tension is resolved, at least for the moment, and The Point is that we must never discount others, because we never know where life's valuable lessons might come from.

Do you remember, back in Step One, that I told you about a retirement lunch I had attended in honor of Edward, a friend of mine who was an anesthesiologist, in which Edward's fellow physician, Ralph, discussed Edward as if he were writing a recommendation on LinkedIn? It started like this:

> In the thirty years that Edward and I have worked together, I have always known him to be a responsible and conscientious professional who gives 100 percent to whatever he undertakes. Edward is organized, resourceful, and devotes painstaking attention to even the most minor details.

The audience sat there with glazed expressions, as Ralph's delivery became more and more urgent in his attempt to persuade people that his approach to this assignment was, in fact, completely sound.

Now, imagine if Ralph had drawn upon the power of storytelling and began his toast with an anecdote. Perhaps it was about the time when Edward and Ralph, attending a conference in London, got utterly lost, and eminently resourceful Edward bailed them out because he knew how to find true north without a compass using the sun. Or about the time when Ralph watched Edward pack his bag with the precision of a mechanical engineer. Such anecdotes could have been used and tied to various aspects of who Edward was (resourceful, painstaking, gives 100 percent to everything). The key would have been for Ralph to figure out which dimensions of Edward he wished to portray and then find the anecdotes to go along with them.

The anecdotes, whether they are long or short and whether there is more than one of them, are all stories, all narratives, and therefore must follow the model that we've been talking about. How was Ralph going to organize the time (i.e., deal with The Once) of the lost-in-London story? What would the extraordinary event be? (Duh. Getting lost.) Where was the conflict and tension? (They had to make a plane? They were due at an important meeting?) And what was The Point? (Edward was someone you could always depend on, and Ralph had become a better person through their association.)

Through the telling of such stories, Ralph's remarks lift off the page and bring illuminating aspects of Edward to life. It is only by drawing on the storytelling ability that I believe lies within all of us that we can make such things happen.

## Up Close

Once again, we are going to "take apart" a piece of writing to see how it evolved, this time keeping the power of storytelling clearly in mind.

Not long ago, I was helping a friend who was working on a letter to the editor for his local newspaper. As this was a small-town newspaper, the bar was not raised particularly high for its letters to the editor, but to my way of thinking there is a right way and a wrong way to do everything, so you might as well do it the right way.

My friend was the chair of a community-action group whose charge was to raise funds to buy musical instruments for students in the school. There had been significant cutbacks in the school budget, and the music program was suffering. My friend wanted his neighbors in town to know about this situation and, hopefully, to join his organization.

Writing such a letter was a simple enough piece of business, you would think, but as you know, things can always take a wrong turn. Here is what his initial draft looked like:

> To the Editor:
>
> As Chairperson of Cherryvale Loves Music, I am writing to affirm my conviction that our town needs to provide all its students with the full range of enrichment opportunities. Our latest school budget showed significant and, in some cases, grievous cuts, particularly in the area of the music curriculum. I believe that the study of music is highly beneficial to students, because it both makes them aware of the power of the arts to elevate the human spirit and fosters the discipline of practice, and we don't want to see that lost.
>
> With the recent budget cuts, many students are going to have to cope with instruments that are badly in need of repair, and many will go without an instrument altogether. This is not fair and is not healthy either for the students or for the community. Cherryvale Loves Music is a not-for-profit, 401(3c) organization founded by citizens of our town with the goal of repairing and purchasing instruments, so that any and all children who wish to study and play music can do so.
>
> On July 5th, we will be hosting a benefit picnic on the grounds of Warren Park and hope that we will be seeing many of our friends and neighbors there. All proceeds will go toward the goal of bringing music into the lives of our children and our community.
>
> Sincerely,
> Arthur Graham

When my friend showed me this draft, my response was that it wasn't badly written, but it just sort of sat there, 200-plus words of predictable prose that was not going to grab anyone's attention. And, of course, grabbing the attention of the public in order to highlight a particular position is the very thing a letter to the editor is supposed to do.

In looking to make this letter more effective, I urged my friend to consider the power of storytelling. His letter consisted mostly of *telling*. Instead, I suggested that we do a bit of *showing*, using storytelling to do that. What is the impact of music on a student's life? That is something we want to see. But our challenge was that we had only 200 words to work with. Was that possible? Here is how the letter changed:

To the Editor:

Sitting on stage, 35 Cherryvale students — intent, expectant, and fully engaged — await the conductor's signal to start. The baton lifts and descends and, as a packed and proud audience watches, those young men and women come together to make exciting music and experience the delights of Béla Bartók's *Hungarian Pictures*.

Last week, as part of an appreciative audience, I felt more convinced than ever of the goals of Cherryvale Loves Music, a not-for-profit, 401(3c) organization founded by citizens of our town. Our goal is to repair and purchase instruments, so that any Cherryvale student who wishes to study and play music can do so. With the recent budget cuts, many students will be using instruments that are badly in need of repair or will go without an instrument altogether. The study of music is highly beneficial, because it both makes students aware of the power of the arts to elevate the human spirit and fosters the discipline of practice, and so we must remedy this situation.

On July 5th, we will be hosting a benefit picnic on the grounds of Warren Park and hope to see many of our friends and neighbors there. All proceeds will go toward the goal of bringing music into the lives of our children and our community through more wonderful concerts, such as the one I was privileged to attend.

Sincerely,

Arthur Graham

Chairperson, Cherryvale Loves Music

So, I'm wondering, which of these two versions do you prefer? I suspect that some of you might say the first — but I am convinced that most people would choose the second. The first is completely by the numbers. There is no spin there, no surprise, nothing for a reader to hook on to. Also, it does not make very good use of its word allotment, if you think of this as having been an assignment of approximately 200 to 250 words. (Most papers have guidelines for the length of their letters to the editor; between 150 and 300 words is a reasonable rule of thumb.)

There is flabbiness in the writing, as there can be in any piece of writing before careful editing takes place, so constructions like "I believe that the study of music is..." simply take up valuable space, when you can easily cut "I believe that" and no one will miss it. Similarly, the very stiff opening — "As Chairperson of Cherryvale Loves Music, I am writing to affirm my conviction" — is not going to capture a reader's attention. In fact, Arthur came to see that he could leave his identification as Chairperson to the signature at the end and thereby save precious words. But those are simply nips and tucks. Of course, it is important to make them — here or in any piece of writing — but they are not going to be game changers. The way this game did change was when we introduced the power of storytelling.

Most people would prefer the second of these two versions, because it brings us into a "story" with a bit of narrative flair. As brief as it is, this tiny story contains the four critical elements of a narrative. The Once, the point in time when the story is told, is in a larger sense at a high-school orchestral concert; in a more focused sense, it is the moment when the baton is about to signal the start of the concert. You also have some sense of The Ordinary vs. the Extraordinary, in that there is a strong feeling of anticipation as the students and the audience await their signal. You have Conflict and Tension, for all of this is set in the context of the underfunding of the music program and what that will mean going forward. And you have The Point, which is that the arts are important and mustn't be sacrificed.

It is interesting to note that these two versions are essentially the same length. Actually, the first version, at 226 words, is exactly the same length as the second, but the second feels far richer and more involving, because it brings us into a story that conveys the emotional underpinnings of the musical experience that Arthur was writing about. Because it has the feeling of a story, it is more likely to lodge in the memory of the reader.

People enjoy stories — they always have and always will. As Philip Pullman said at the beginning of this step, "After nourishment, shelter, and companionship, stories are the thing we need most in the world." Even if you would balk at putting stories in fourth place, you must admit they rank high. And now that you have a better sense of how the power of storytelling can be used, it is there for you to use.

## ROUNDUP

1. The four critical elements of a narrative are The Once, The Ordinary vs. the Extraordinary, Conflict and Tension, and The Point.
2. The Once is the writer's solution to how to structure the time within a narrative.
3. The Extraordinary is the unusual event that ignites the action of the narrative and wrests it away from the Ordinary.
4. Tension and Conflict are the elements that create a context for the narrative.
5. Conflict can occur between individuals, between groups, between individuals and society, between individuals and their internal forces, between individuals and nature, and more.
6. The Point makes it clear why a reader has been asked to spend time with a narrative.
7. The power of storytelling can help infuse life into many different writing assignments that might initially have been approached in a more formulaic way.

## STEP FOUR

# Revel in the Amazing, Expandable, Elastic, Evolving Sentence

In her book *The Writing Life*, the author Annie Dillard shares the story of a fellow writer's encounter with one of his students. The student asks the writer whether he thinks that he, the student, might also become a writer one day, and the writer responds by saying, "Well, do you like sentences?" That story prompts Dillard's own memory of a time when she asked a friend who was a painter how he came to be one. "I like the smell of paint," her artist friend replied.

Both of these stories convey the message that raw materials often lie at the heart of expressive work, whether it is painting, writing, cooking, or flower arranging. You begin with the fundamentals, and you love the fundamentals.

I do. I love sentences. I love sentences for the way they can be altered and amended. I love sentences for the way they can wander down mysterious and labyrinthine byways, never getting lost, so long as there is a basic understanding of the structure of the sentence and how it works.

There. You just read four sentences in a row that were noticeably different from the ones that preceded them. You can do that with sentences. You can turn them inside out, upside down, and front to back. The only hard and fast rules are that your sentence must always begin with a capital letter (unless you're e. e. cummings), always end with a period (unless you're e. e. cummings), and always contain a subject and a predicate (to be explained momentarily). But let's not worry so much right now about rules. Let's focus on the fact that sentences are fun. Sentences are challenging. Sentences are challenging and fun.

According to Bookfox, a blog about writing, the longest sentence in English literature is 13,955 words (that's approximately 55 book pages, if you use the industry standard of 250 words per page). It can be found in a book you may never have heard of called *The Rotters' Club*, by the English writer Jonathan Coe. The runner-up is said to be from a book you probably have heard of: *Ulysses*, by James Joyce. There you will find a sentence of 4,391 words (approximately 17 book pages). Let me calm you, however. *You will never be asked to write a sentence that long.*

Some writers, like Joyce, William Faulkner, and Henry James, are famous (or infamous, depending on how you look at it) for using forbiddingly long sentences, which rules them out for casual readers, who may be unwilling to put in the effort required to discover the splendors of exalted literary creation. It can be instructive, however, to examine an unusually long sentence (by *unusually long*, I mean in the range of

100 words) to see how a writer can manipulate language while maintaining perfect mastery of form.

E. B. White was a great American writer whose 1918 book on writing, *The Elements of Style*, written with William Strunk, Jr., has been a bestseller for almost a century. White is also famous for his two great works of children's literature, *Charlotte's Web* and *Stuart Little*. In the latter, there is a sentence of 107 words — and one can only imagine what a contemporary publisher would say if a children's book author turned in a manuscript with a 107-word sentence. "Are you insane?" we can hear the publisher roar. "No child's attention could be held by such a sentence."

In fact, legions of children have fallen in love with *Stuart Little* ever since its publication in 1945 — even with that very long sentence. Let's have a look at it:

> In the loveliest town of all, where the houses were white and high and the elm trees were green and higher than the houses, where the front yards were wide and pleasant and the back yards were bushy and worth finding out about, where the streets sloped down to the stream and the stream flowed quietly under the bridge, where the lawns ended in orchards and the orchards ended in fields and the fields ended in pastures and the pastures climbed the hill and disappeared over the top toward the wonderful wide sky, in this loveliest of all towns Stuart stopped to get a drink of sarsaparilla.

A beautiful sentence — and one that very few people would dare to write. Certainly, it is unlikely that a less than confident writer would dare to write such a sentence because, if she tried, she would surely hear an army of English teachers telling her that she couldn't. "It's a run-on sentence!" you can hear them screaming. "Don't go there!"

In fact, it's not a run-on sentence. It's a very long sentence. There is a difference.

E. B. White chose to write this very long sentence for a reason. The reason is not because he ran out of periods that day. The reason is because he wanted to create a certain mood and decided that this sentence, with its virtual cataract of imagery, all expressed in the clear, direct language for which White was known, was the right vehicle for that mood.

Now here's a sentence from the novel *Sula*, by Nobel laureate Toni Morrison, that was chosen by the editors of *The American Scholar* as one of the "ten best sentences." At 24 words, it's less than one-quarter of the length of the E. B. White sentence, but it carries enormous punch for that length:

> It was a fine cry — loud and long — but it had no bottom and it had no top, just circles and circles of sorrow.

As a writer, I look at that sentence and think about the choices that Morrison made. "It was a fine cry." The word *fine* resonates in that sentence, because there is something intrinsically ironic in its juxtaposition with the "circles and circles of sorrow" at the end of the sentence. That juxtaposition creates a tension that arrests readers' attention. If Morrison had written, "It was a painful cry," then nothing much would be happening. In fact, the word *painful* would have felt painfully obvious. Then you have the appositive phrase — "loud and long" — set off by long dashes. That phrase momentarily stops readers so that they can think even more about that fine cry and conjure up its pain.

Then you have the choice of words that follow the appositive phrase: "it had no bottom and it had no top." Morrison might have said, "it had no bottom and no top." Why then did she repeat the words *it had*? Was it to create a strong parallelism? To me, this sentence evoking a cry of pain feels like a blackbird circling in the sky. I go instantaneously from reading it to seeing it — and that is what makes it such a great sentence. Morrison created this great sentence by making choices all along the way, just as you will be making choices when you sit down to write your sentences.

Before you make such choices, however, you need to have a clear sense of how sentences are constructed.

## Structuring Sentences

Thinking back to my early English classes, so many years ago, I can still recapture the dread I experienced when confronted with the pedagogical approach to teaching sentence structure that was in favor at that time. It was all about diagramming.

In theory, diagramming sentences seems like a relatively good idea. The idea was to create an easily recognizable visual representation of the relationship of the critical parts of a sentence. And in an easy sentence like "The runner stumbled" the diagram is very clear:

Runner | stumbled.

What happens, however, when you have a sentence like this? "Jogging along the briar path, the runner hit a pothole and, losing his balance, stumbled into the bushes." The diagram starts to look like an aerial view of an LA freeway, and insight gives way to panic.

The idea for this kind of diagramming was hatched back in 1877, when two professors at Brooklyn Polytechnic Institute, Alonzo Reed and Brainerd Kellogg, thought that this graphic approach would be the answer to the challenge of teaching sentence structure. Their approach swept the country and lasted for about a hundred years before it fell into disfavor. Today, it is all but lost. The Common Core, the 2010 nationwide initiative setting English and math standards for all students K–12, doesn't even refer to it. Nowadays, the prevailing approach to teaching sentence structure has less to do with rules and resoundingly more to do with *having students read and write.*

In a study titled "The Role of Grammar in a Secondary School Curriculum," released in 1979, researcher W. B. Elley and colleagues followed three groups of students from ninth to eleventh grade. One group had a curriculum that was based on rules, a second received an alternative approach to grammar instruction, and a third had classes that emphasized literature and creative writing and contained no grammar lessons at all. The findings showed that there were no significant differences among the three groups with regard to the students' ability to master sentence structure — but the two grammar groups came away with a distinct aversion for English.

If you have a history of not liking English, now is the time to try to put aside that history and aim for a fresh start, because chances are that your negative associations are going to keep you from making good sentences. Remember what Annie Dillard said to the aspiring writer: "Do you like sentences?" The goal of anyone who wants to learn to write well is to learn to like sentences.

As I mentioned at the beginning of this book, I often see marked improvement in a student's writing after we have worked together for as little as a week or two. That applies even to my STEM students who claim no interest or affection for the written word. How can that be? Well, in all modesty, I think it has something to do with being intimately and intensely connected, even for a short time, to a person (like myself) who passionately loves sentences. Even with all the pressures of application deadlines, a sense of delight enters into the work, and that delight is very much about the commitment and care we give to our product. We pore over every word, scrutinize every comma, and make sentences that may not be as beautiful as those that Toni Morrison makes, but are considerably more beautiful than the sentences that these students are used to making.

As I said earlier in this book, very few of my student writers have a genuine gift for writing. Out of the many hundreds of students I have worked with, very few have struck me as naturally gifted writers. Most of my students fall into the very broad middle of the pack. They have some sense of sentence structure, so things rarely get disastrous, but nonetheless their sentences can be plodding, lackluster, and forgettable. Then there are those students whose sense of sentence structure is completely lacking, and in such cases we must go back to basics. Going back to basics, however, is not a bad idea for anyone who wants to learn how to write better sentences.

## The Basics

One thing you may have forgotten from your early English classes — or one thing that you may never have known — is that even though the English language has countless words, it has, in fact, only eight parts of speech. Parts of speech are those categories of words that have similar grammatical properties and will generally behave in a consistent way when it comes to *syntax*, which is the arrangement of words and phrases to create well-formed sentences. A verb, for instance, conveys action. An adjective describes a noun. An adverb describes a verb. And so on. Here are the eight parts of speech.

### Nouns

A noun is a word for a person, place, thing, or idea (*mother, New Jersey, watermelon, democracy*). A noun is often accompanied by an article — *a, an,* or *the* — but can stand alone as well (as in the case of *Mother, New Jersey,* and *Democracy*). Proper nouns — names (*Derek Jeter, Katy Perry, Santa Claus, Boston*) — are always capitalized.

### Pronouns

Pronouns were invented to replace nouns. Without pronouns, a given piece of text might read like this:

Franklin Roosevelt was the thirty-second president of the United States. Franklin Roosevelt was born in 1882 in Hyde Park, New York. Franklin Roosevelt graduated from Harvard in 1903.

With pronouns, the text becomes more pleasant for readers, primarily because it saves them precious time:

Franklin Roosevelt was the thirty-second president of the United States. He was born in 1882 in Hyde Park, New York. He graduated from Harvard in 1903.

Some examples of common pronouns, as I'm sure you know, are *I*, *we*, *they*, *she*, *he*, and *it*.

## Verbs

Verbs are the engines of the sentence. They express action or a state of being (*sing*, *dance*, *think*, *be*). Verbs can have helping verbs — "I can sing" is an example of a sentence in which *sing* is the main verb and *can* (or *will* or *won't* or *could* or *should*) is the helping verb. Verbs take different forms based on tense, or the time of the action (*bring*, *brought*, *will bring*; *run*, *ran*, *will run*).

## Adjectives

The purpose of an adjective is to modify (tell you more about) a noun, ostensibly making it clearer, prettier, more intense, and so on. In the sentence "She carried a colorful parasol," the word *colorful* functions as an adjective. It modifies the word *parasol*, presumably making it more vivid. We will talk about adjectives later in this book, but in general I'm not a fan of them. They are overused and often unnecessary and can clog up your writing.

## Adverbs

As an adjective modifies a noun, an adverb modifies a verb. In the sentence "I walked quickly to the store," the adverb *quickly* modifies the verb *walked*. The same warning applies to adverbs as to adjectives. They are overused and can bring down the level of your writing. More about that later.

## Prepositions

A preposition is a handy little word — *by*, *with*, *from*, *over*, *under* (and many, many others) — that, when placed before a noun or a pronoun, creates a prepositional phrase. A prepositional phrase modifies other words in the sentence. For example, "Our group had a good discussion about the book" is a sentence in which *about the book* is a prepositional phrase that modifies the noun *discussion*. "The boat sailed down the river" is another example, in which *down the river* is a prepositional phrase that modifies a verb, this time *sailed*. Essentially, prepositional phrases act like adjectives or adverbs, modifying nouns and verbs.

## Conjunctions

Conjunctions form the connective tissue that joins words (in "apples and oranges" the *and* serves as the conjunction) as well as phrases and clauses ("Apples and oranges should not be compared, but many people make that mistake"; here the word *but* is joining two distinct clauses).

## Interjections

Stop! We can't leave this section without citing those parts of speech, usually accompanied by exclamation points (and just about the only place where exclamation points are forgiven), that express emotions like surprise, shock, pain, and outrage. *Oh! Ow! Ooh!* That sort of thing.

So forgive me if this all seems way too granular for you, but many of us don't store such information in our brains. Let's just say that having a firm grasp of the parts of speech will help you understand the overall logic of sentences. Now let's move on to those two must-haves that no sentence can be without: a subject and a predicate.

## Subjects and Predicates

Even if you've heard this at other points in your life, let's say it again. Every sentence must have a subject, which is the person or the thing that connects to the action, that is, the predicate, otherwise thought of as the verb (although not all verbs are predicates). "I eat" is a perfectly acceptable and correct sentence, because it has a subject, *I*, and a predicate, *eat*. Is it a prizewinner of a sentence? Of course not. It sounds like something that some brute might say while gnawing on a mutton chop. Even so, as a sentence there is absolutely nothing wrong with it.

A problem I see with some of my writers is that they lose the sense of the subject and the predicate. By the time they finish writing their tangled and mangled sentences, the subject and the predicate are just like any other two words in the sentence rather than the drivers of the bus.

You want to be absolutely clear that the subject and the predicate are the drivers of your bus. How do you manage to do that? Well, if you are not yet a fully confident writer, you do it by placing your subject and predicate at the beginning of your sentences.

Let's look at a sentence in which subject and predicate get lost. Here is one from a college admission essay by one of my students:

> From this experience although I have grown distraught over atrocities in the world, I have become a tad bit wiser and knowledgeable of who I am and what I want to do on the rest of my journey called life.

This bus is clearly going through the guardrail, off the road, and down the cliff. The real culprit here is the logjam of phrases at the beginning. The writer starts with a prepositional phrase — "From this experience" — and then moves directly into a conjunction, "although," to introduce another phrase about having grown distraught over atrocities in the world. It is not until readers are nearly halfway into the sentence that they discover the subject, "I," and the predicate, "have become."

There is, of course, other problematic writing in this sentence. I don't know that anyone should ever use the expression "a tad bit." And the "journey called life"? You could call that a *bathetic* expression. Good word, *bathetic*, meaning having the quality of *bathos*, which is both "exceptional commonplaceness or triteness" and "insincere or overdone pathos." Be sure to collect new words. They will help your writing enormously if you genuinely understand and know how to use them.

"But I don't want to lose the first part of my sentence!" I can imagine my student crying.

All right, I hear you. But let's see how we can hold on to what you have while still crafting something intelligible.

The "experience" to which the student was referring was a trip she took with her family to Hungary to visit the birthplace of her father. There, she became viscerally aware of the impact of the Holocaust as it affected both her own family history and modern European history. So then, to place the problematic sentence within the context of its paragraph, here is what it looks like when accompanied by the preceding sentence:

> The conductor announces over the loud microphone that we will soon reach our final destination and I recognize the physical and mental journey that I have just embarked on. From this experience although I have grown distraught over atrocities in the world, I have become a tad bit wiser and knowledgeable of who I am and what I want to do on the rest of my journey called life.

Problems emerge for this less than confident writer in that first sentence as well. ("The loud microphone"? Microphones aren't innately loud or soft; they are pieces of equipment that can be adjusted to be loud or soft. "Embarked on"? *Embarkation* suggests the point of departure, not the journey in its entirety, which is what she is talking about if she is just about to reach her destination.)

But, in any case, you see the context now. So let's re-imagine the final paragraph of this student's essay and see where it might go, as I show my editing marks on the draft:

> ~~The~~ As the conductor announces over the ~~loud~~ micro-phone that we will soon reach our ~~final~~ destination, ~~and~~ I think about ~~recognize~~ the physical and mental jour-ney ~~that~~ I have ~~just embarked~~been on. It has made me wiser and more knowledgeable about who I am, even as I have sometimes grown distraught over the atroci-ties to which I have been exposed.~~From this experience although I have grown distraught over atrocities in the world, I have become a tad bit wiser and knowledgeable of who I am and what I want to do on the rest of my journey called life.~~

Although the first sentence of that paragraph was clean enough to allow us to disregard the rule for starting with a subject and a predicate, the second sentence became hope-lessly tangled, so we had to go back to basics. Now that sec-ond sentence starts with the subject, "It" (the physical and mental journey that the writer has been on), and predicate, "has made." The problematic opening from the original ver-sion has been moved to the latter half of the sentence where it is no longer problematic — meaning that no one, neither writer nor reader, will get lost in it. (In fact, four drafts later, this whole paragraph disappeared and was replaced by some-thing new, but hey — that's writing for you.)

Confident and seasoned writers do not have to play by

the rule of placing subject and predicate at the beginning of sentences. I have been a professional writer for four decades and, most of that time, a reasonably confident one, and so, as you can see from the book you're reading, I am not leading every one of my sentences with a subject and a predicate. I would like you to know, however, that there is absolutely nothing wrong with doing so. When I work with writers, I always stress that a reader will never hold good, clean, simple language against you. Readers are sure to resent writers, however, whose sentence structure is as tangled as last year's Christmas tree lights. The work of untangling is time-consuming and should not fall upon the reader. Such untangling is the job of the writer.

One need look no farther than Ernest Hemingway to examine the work of a writer who gained acclaim with a style that was essentially based on simplicity. Consider these opening sentences from his classic novel *The Sun Also Rises*:

> Robert Cohn was once middleweight boxing champion of Princeton. Do not think that I am very much impressed by that as a boxing title, but it meant a lot to Cohn. He cared nothing for boxing, in fact he disliked it, but he learned it painfully and thoroughly to counteract the feeling of inferiority and shyness he had felt on being treated as a Jew at Princeton. There was a certain inner comfort in knowing he could knock down anybody who was snooty to him, although, being very shy and a thoroughly nice boy, he never fought except in the gym. He was Spider Kelly's star pupil. Spider Kelly taught all his young gentlemen to box like featherweights, no matter whether they weighed one

hundred and five or two hundred and five pounds. But it seemed to fit Cohn. He was really very fast.

Note that most of the sentences in this paragraph feature a noun and a verb *right at the beginning*. "Robert Cohn was..." "Do not think..." (the implied subject here is "you," the reader, as in "You should not think..."). "He cared..." "He was..." "Spider Kelly taught..." "He was..."

Hemingway's style proved to be an earthquake on the literary landscape of his time and has been profoundly influential ever since, no matter what one thinks of the overall merit of his work. He drew on his background as a journalist to forge a style that was based on several key features: (1) an emphasis on nouns and verbs rather than adjectives and adverbs; (2) a reliance on recognizable vocabulary; and (3) short sentences, or at least longer sentences that were composed of short phrases and clauses joined by conjunctions. His style was not viewed as simplistic, but rather as a force of modernism that blew away all that had come before. It was, in other words, the literary equivalent of the Bauhaus design concepts that replaced the overstuffed furniture, beaded lampshades, flocked wallpaper, and overall clutter of the Victorian era with natural light, natural forms, and overall minimalism.

To understand the revolution that Hemingway started, one need only look at this sentence from Henry James's novel *The Ambassadors*, which was published twenty-three years before *The Sun Also Rises*:

The principle I have just mentioned as operating had been, with the most newly disembarked of the two men, wholly instinctive — the fruit of a sharp sense that, delightful as it would be to find himself looking, after so much separation, into his comrade's face, his business would be a trifle bungled should he simply arrange for this countenance to present itself to the nearing steamer as the first "note" of Europe.

Although Henry James was undeniably a great artist, such sentences make his work quite inaccessible to many people. (Great art is not judged on accessibility, however.) So then, given the fact that literature welcomed the simple sentences of Hemingway, clearly your readers will be able to do the same if you need to rely on simple sentence structure, at least to start out. And, once again, that simple sentence structure is based on the premise of *subjects and predicates at the beginning of sentences*.

Here is another problematic sentence from a student essay that I worked on:

As a first-generation Asian American, there is usually a need for a balancing act between my Chinese roots and the proud American culture I live in to create the confidence that fits me.

In many respects, this is a mess. The opening clause, "As a first-generation Asian American," requires that a personal pronoun follow it. "As a first-generation Asian American, *I* feel the need..." or "*I* am compelled..." or "*I* must balance..." Following that first clause with the phrase "there is usually a need" is very clumsy writing. It is writing, in fact, that conveys a noticeable lack of confidence. When confidence is in short supply, a writer is likely to form such fusty locutions in an effort to sound more "important." (And if you're collecting vocabulary words, *fusty* is not a bad one to have at your disposal. It means both "stale, damp, or stuffy" and "old-fashioned in attitude and style.")

Moving ahead with this problematic sentence, we have that last clause, "to create the confidence that fits me," which has no relation to anything else in the sentence and is quite inscrutable in its meaning. It's just tacked on — and, oddly enough, the writer wasn't even sure why he tacked it on.

The whole sentence needed to be unpacked, rearranged, and rewritten. And we soon realized that it didn't have to be one sentence. Here is what we came up with:

> I have grown up as a first-generation Asian American. My life has been a balancing act between my Chinese roots and the American culture in which I live. I work hard to resolve that conflict, so I can attain the confidence I need to succeed.

In the process of rewriting, we relied on the principle of subject and predicate at the beginning of sentences: "I have grown up...," "My life has been...," "I work hard..." My student understood that his readers would be perfectly okay with this kind of structure. They wouldn't hold such structure against him, simple as it was, as much as they would punish him for the tangled writing that characterized his first draft. Let's say it again: *No one ever resents good, clean, muscular writing.*

As this student and I kept at the work, however, he came to see that he could begin to mix up his sentences, for now he had a stronger grasp on sentence structure. He could experiment and play around with his sentence structure, because the rule we had set down — *subject and predicate at the beginning of the sentence* — made everything that much clearer.

## Objects

Once again, the goal of this chapter is to serve up a kind of crash course on sentence structure. Yes, everyone should know all this by now, but many, many people don't. Either they never got it straight in the first place, they have lost the thread over the years, they come out of another language tradition, or who knows why.

By now, you understand that every sentence must have a subject and a predicate. Without both of those in place, there is no sentence. "I eat" is a sentence. "Eat!" is also a sentence, as it is a command with an implied subject (you) and a predicate (*eat*): "(You) eat!" "I" by itself is not a sentence. There is no action, explicit or implicit, connected with that word.

Every sentence must have a subject that is connected to some form of action, but a sentence is also likely to contain an object. There are two kinds of objects: *direct* and *indirect*. A direct object, which receives the action of the sentence, is typically a noun or a pronoun. Let's look at a sentence from those opening lines of *The Sun Also Rises*:

> Spider Kelly taught all his young gentlemen to box like featherweights, no matter whether they weighed one hundred and five or two hundred and five pounds.

Given our mastery of subjects and predicates (which I am counseling you to place at the beginnings of your sentences, at least often enough to have a firm sense of control), we know that the subject is *Spider Kelly* and the predicate is *taught*. The direct object is *all his young gentlemen*. According to our definition of a direct object, these young gentlemen are receiving the action of the sentence. They are being *taught* (predicate) by *Spider Kelly* (subject).

Again, direct objects receive the action of the sentence:

The man walked his dog.

The postal carrier delivered the letter.

Abigail read a story.

In those three sentences, the direct objects are, respectively, *his dog*, *the letter*, and *a story*. They are receiving the action (*walked*, *delivered*, *read*) performed by the subject (*the man*, *the postal carrier*, *Abigail*). Now let's move on to the other kind of object: the indirect object.

The role of an indirect object is more difficult to explain than the role of a direct object. The indirect object is the person or entity for whom the action of the sentence is being performed. Here are some examples of indirect objects, noted in bold text, in three different sentences:

The man offered **his dog** a bone.

The postal carrier gave **Mrs. Johnson** her letter.

Abigail read **her daughter** a story.

As before, we have the three building blocks of a sentence: the subject; the predicate, or action; and the direct object, which receives the action. But now we also have an indirect object — the person or entity that is receiving the direct object after the direct object receives the action (predicate) from the subject. The indirect object always goes between the verb (predicate) and the direct object. Often an indirect object can be replaced by a prepositional phrase. Our examples above could be written like this:

The man offered a bone **to his dog**.

The postal carrier gave a letter **to Mrs. Johnson**.

Abigail read a story **to her daughter**.

Is it better to write a sentence so that you have an indirect object instead of a prepositional phrase? There is no hard answer to that question. Mostly, it's a matter of ear or, otherwise put, what sounds good to you. In the famous words of Duke Ellington, quoted in all my books on writing, "If it sounds good, it is good." Is it surprising that one of our greatest jazz musicians should have something so apt to say about writing? Not really. Let's not forget that writing is an aural experience. The writer and the reader "hear" these words, even if they are never spoken aloud.

## Sentence Variations

Although the whole point of this book is to inspire confidence in you as a writer and the thrust of this chapter is to help you understand that sentences are flexible creations that can be rewarding to work with when you understand sentence structure, let us also admit that sentences can go wrong in many ways. Whew. Now, that was a complex sentence. (Or was it a compound-complex one?) But before we talk about problems like sentence fragments and run-on sentences, we need to discuss some basic architecture.

If you are familiar with the forms that sentences take, then you can vary your sentence structure, which makes for a more interesting experience for your readers (and for you, the writer). All sentences fall into one of four categories:

- Simple
- Compound
- Complex
- Compound-complex

Your understanding of these four types of sentences depends largely on your understanding of clauses. A *clause* is a part of a sentence that has its own subject and verb. There are two types of clauses: *independent* and *dependent*. Let's look again at a piece of text from one of my students that I shared earlier:

As the conductor announces over the microphone that we will soon reach our destination, I think about the physical and mental journey I have been on. It has made me wiser and more knowledgeable about who I am, even as I have sometimes grown distraught over the atrocities to which I have been exposed.

You can see that the first and second sentences are each made up of two clauses. In the first sentence, the clause "I think about the physical and mental journey I have been on" would make a perfectly fine sentence by itself. It has a subject (*I*) and a predicate (*think*). In the second, the clause "It has made me wiser and more knowledgeable about who I am" could also be its own sentence, with its own subject (*It*) and its own predicate (*has made*). Both of those clauses are *independent*, for all independent clauses can stand on their own.

It is perfectly legitimate for a sentence to be made up of more than one independent clause. For instance, look what happens if I rewrite that first sentence this way:

> I think about the physical and mental journey I have been on, and the conductor announces over the microphone that we will soon reach our destination.

In that treatment, you have two independent clauses that are joined by the conjunction *and*. The two clauses are equal in the sense that both of those clauses can stand on their own as complete sentences: "I think about the physical and mental journey I have been on." "The conductor announces over the microphone that we will soon reach our destination."

So then, two independent clauses are joined by the conjunction *and* to make up one sentence. All is good, yes? Then why not use independent clauses all the time and not bother with *subordinate* (*dependent*) clauses, clauses that cannot stand on their own two feet and need an independent clause to lean on? Well, the reason for not always using independent clauses is that you might want to convey something about the relationship between the clauses, some kind of causality, let's say, that wouldn't get expressed simply by stringing together independent clauses.

Look again at that sentence:

> I think about the physical and mental journey I have been on, and the conductor announces over the microphone that we will soon reach our destination.

There is not much of a relationship, if any, between those two clauses. But in the version that my student ultimately went with, there is a relationship:

> As the conductor announces over the microphone that we will soon reach our destination, I think about the physical and mental journey I have been on.

It is a subtle relationship, but it's there. The feeling is that amid the "background noise" generated by the conductor, the subject (*I*) goes deeper into her thinking.

Her move into deeper thinking becomes the "driver" of the sentence. In other words, that is where the importance of that sentence lies, compared with the first part of the sentence, which provides the setting. In order to have the sentence deliver the meaning we wanted, we established the relationship between the clauses by turning the first into a subordinate clause. As a subordinate clause, it cannot stand on its own. If you say it aloud — "As the conductor announces over the microphone that we will soon reach our destination" — it feels unfinished, as if you're waiting for the second shoe to drop, doesn't it?

When an independent clause is joined with a subordinate clause, that act of joining is accomplished by using a *subordinating conjunction*. It will be easier for me to show you the subordinating conjunction in the sentence we've just been examining if I flip the clauses:

> I think about the physical and mental journey I have been on, as the conductor announces over the microphone that we will soon reach our destination.

*As* is the subordinating conjunction, and by using it in this sentence we have created a subordinate clause. Common subordinating conjunctions are words like *although*, *after*, *because*, *since*, *before*, *once*, *where*, and *while* as well as short phrases like *even if*, *even though*, *in order that*, and *rather than*.

When you gain a grasp of independent and subordinate clauses, you can better understand the whole matter of sentence variation. As we said a few moments ago, all sentences fall into one of four categories: simple, compound, complex, and compound-complex.

## Simple Sentences

A simple sentence is made up of only one independent clause. "Jack did his homework." It has a subject (*Jack*), a predicate (*did*), and an object (*homework*). It stands on its own — uninspired perhaps, but sturdy.

## Compound Sentences

Compound sentences are also easy enough. If you join two simple sentences with a conjunction, you get a compound sentence. "Sadie likes broccoli, and she also likes cauliflower." Variations on such a sentence, featuring different conjunctions, might sound like this: "Sadie likes broccoli, but she doesn't like cauliflower," or "Sadie likes broccoli, so naturally she likes cauliflower."

A semicolon, which is probably the most misused punctuation in existence, can be used correctly in this situation, separating two independent but related clauses. So you might say, "Sadie likes broccoli; she also likes cauliflower." You would not say, "Sadie likes broccoli; broccoli grows on stalks." Those two thoughts are completely unrelated and cannot be connected that way. We'll talk later about semicolons, but it's probably best to steer clear of them in general because, as I say, they are so often misused.

## Complex Sentences

Complex sentences contain both a dependent and an independent clause. Both clauses contain subjects and verbs, but the dependency of the dependent clause is made evident by the presence of the subordinating conjunction (*although*, *because*, *since*, *where*, as we discussed above). Here is that sentence again, rendered complex this time: "Even though Sadie likes broccoli, she doesn't like cauliflower." The first part cannot stand on its own — remember that "second shoe waiting to drop" sensation? — so it is dependent, *even though* it has a subject and verb. (Note the use of *even though* in the sentence I just wrote, rendering that clause dependent.)

Note too the use of the comma after the opening clause,

"Even though Sadie likes broccoli." If you were to flip the sentence, putting the dependent clause after the independent clause — "Sadie doesn't like cauliflower even though she likes broccoli" — then you would not need a comma before *even though*.

### Compound-Complex Sentences

Remember that Henry James text? That was a supreme version of a compound-complex sentence. In such a sentence, which you may not want to try for a while, there are at least two independent clauses and one dependent clause.

A compound-complex sentence might look like this:

Although Sadie likes broccoli, she doesn't enjoy cauliflower, and she always avoids it when she can.

There you have two independent clauses — "she doesn't enjoy cauliflower" and "she always avoids it when she can" — with a dependent clause leading the sentence ("Although Sadie likes broccoli").

Compound-complex sentences add a certain complexity to a piece of text and convey a sense of rich writing. Down the line, it will be good to take on such sentences, even though they can be something of a minefield. Again, however, that is down the line. You will get no demerits if your writing does not feature compound-complex sentences. You will, however, get demerits for compound-complex sentences that are riddled with errors.

Now that we know that *all* sentences fall into one of these four categories — simple sentences, compound sentences, complex sentences, and compound-complex sentences — we can discuss some of the more common problems that afflict them.

## Sentences Gone Wrong

Sentences can go wrong in an infinite number of ways, but three mishaps are especially prevalent. These are fragments, run-on sentences, and comma splices.

### Fragments

A sentence fragment is a group of words that fails to become a sentence because it lacks one or more of the three things that make up a sentence: a subject, a verb that goes along with the subject, and a completed thought. Fragments happen all the time in spoken language — "Wait a minute, did I...?" — but no one looks at us funny when they come out of our mouths. In fact, if every one of our sentences was an impeccably constructed jewel, then people might indeed look at us funny.

In written work, however, fragments are telltale signs of inexperienced writing. The good news is that they are relatively easy to spot if you read your work aloud. "Likes broccoli but hates cauliflower" obviously doesn't sound like a sentence, because it's lacking a subject (*Sadie*). "Even though Sadie" is obviously not a sentence, because it lacks a verb. "Even though Sadie likes broccoli" has a subject and a verb (*Sadie*, *likes*), but it is a fragment because it does not complete a thought.

## Run-on Sentences

Run-ons are another sign of inexperienced writers. They show a serious lack of knowledge about punctuation. I have seen run-on sentences that look like these:

The patient was sick he was close to death.

The dog jumped he was chasing a ball.

The pizza got cold it didn't taste good.

In all three of these examples, some form of punctuation is called for, because in each instance you essentially have two complete sentences that are incorrectly jammed together.

Here are the sentences correctly punctuated:

The patient was sick, and he was close to death.

The dog jumped; he was chasing a ball.

The pizza got cold, and it didn't taste good.

In the first instance, we see the correct use of a semicolon, which is to join two independent clauses to form a compound sentence. (Remember, you can only do that when there is some meaningful relationship between the clauses. You couldn't write, for instance, "The patient was sick; he was born in Cincinnati." There is no kind of logical connection between those two clauses, so a semicolon will not work.)

In the second instance, you have a complex sentence in which the independent clause ("The dog jumped") is joined to the dependent clause ("while he was chasing a ball") using the subordinating conjunction *while*. No comma is necessary before the word *while*. If you were to flip the sentence, however, and had the dependent clause first ("While he was chasing a ball, the dog jumped"), then you would need a comma after the dependent clause, as shown.

## Comma Splices

Comma splices are quite easy to explain, as they are simply a variation on the run-on sentence. In such cases, the writer simply inserts a comma between the two independent clauses, like so:

> The patient was sick, he was close to death.
>
> The dog jumped, he was chasing a ball.
>
> The pizza got cold, it didn't taste good.

That is entirely wrong, so don't do it.

## Mixing It Up

There has been a lot to absorb from this lesson, and I regret to say that I cannot assure you that your writing will be flawless even if you have mastered all the information provided herein. There are many more important technical issues connected with writing that we will discuss as we go along. And then there are less important but still significant issues like dangling participles and an overreliance on gerunds, let's say, that we will not have adequate time to discuss in this book.

That said, I have attempted to give you an overview of sentence structure, so that what may seem overwhelming at first can, in fact, come to be seen as something that can be organized and learned. There are eight parts of speech. There are two must-haves for any sentence: a subject and a predicate. There are two kinds of clauses. There are four kinds of sentences. Those rules, if we must use that word, are not overwhelming, people. And once you have that kind of overview, then you can get into the fun part of writing, which is to vary your sentences.

Think back to Ernest Hemingway, who reclaimed the power of the simple sentence. However, if you go back to look at that brief excerpt from *The Sun Also Rises*, you will see that he used all four kinds of sentences, mixing them up, so that he offered readers relief from any feeling of sameness that can afflict a piece of prose.

He also recognized, as skilled writers do, that each sentence has its own integrity. As a writer, I have kept in mind the image of the sentence as a wave. Each sentence rolls in, crests in a certain place, and then rolls out. Each sentence has a rhythm of its own, each paragraph has a rhythm of its own, and if you are an extremely skilled writer, even a novel can have a rhythm of its own. Now that you understand the basics, perhaps you will begin to hear that rhythm.

## Up Close

As this has been quite a long step, our Up Close can be a short one. Let's just look at a cover letter that was submitted for a job application and see how it evolved, focusing primarily on sentence structure.

> Dear Hiring Manager,*
> I am writing with regard to your advertisement for a marketing assistant. I believe I am a qualified candidate. I earned a business degree from the University of Maryland in May. I took marketing courses there. They included Customer-Centric Innovation, Introduction to Logistics and Supply Chain Management, and Integrated Marketing Communications. I believe I fulfill the qualifications listed in the advertisement. These include: a solid educational foundation, technological acumen, a proven ability to interact with people from diverse backgrounds, and a track record of excellent performance in assorted internships. I would very much like to meet with you. I could share more of my qualifications. I could also learn more about your needs. Please feel free to call me at (201) 972-1845 or email at raoul.webb@gmail.com.
> Thank you for reviewing the enclosed résumé. I look forward to hearing from you.
> Sincerely,
> Raoul Webb

This writer labored over this letter for many hours, and I commended him for his commitment. In fact, he wound up

---

\*    Note: This sounded a little weird to my ears, but apparently in a survey of two thousand employers Saddleback College found out that 40 percent preferred this salutation rather than "Dear Sir or Madam" or "To Whom It May Concern" when receiving correspondence from unknown senders.

with a letter that had no technical errors, which is always a pleasure. On the other hand, all the sentences were lined up like little tin soldiers in a row. There was no variety to the sentence structure; instead, the impression was a stultifying sense of sameness. I assured him that some employers might not hold that against him, but why not make it livelier? Easy enough to do, I explained, just by varying the sentence structure. (I am totally going to ignore content in this example. Ultimately, we did adjust some of it, but I want to stay focused only on sentence structure here.)

Here is what this same letter looked like when the writer mixed up his sentences, calling on all four varieties of sentences to give the letter movement and vigor:

Dear Hiring Manager,

Your recent advertisement for a marketing assistant captured my attention, and I am convinced that I am well qualified for this position. In earning a business degree at the University of Maryland, from which I graduated in May, I took a full slate of marketing courses. These included Customer-Centric Innovation, Introduction to Logistics and Supply Chain Management, and Integrated Marketing Communications, all of which I found fascinating and which prepared me well for the position you have listed.

In line with the qualifications you are seeking in a candidate, I can claim a solid educational foundation, good technological acumen, a proven ability to interact with people from diverse backgrounds, and a track record of excellent performance in assorted internships. All of this is reflected in the attached résumé.

I am hoping that we can meet in person, so that I

can share more of my qualifications with you and learn more about your needs. Please feel free to call me at (201) 972-1845 or email at raoul.webb@gmail.com.

Thank you for reviewing the enclosed résumé. I look forward to hearing from you.

Sincerely,

Raoul Webb

As you can see, the letter now contains a lively mix of sentence types, with compound, complex, and compound-complex varieties. It ends with two simple sentences, which also works well, as the simplicity at the end conveys a forcefulness that reflects well on the writer.

If you are now wondering how you are ever going to achieve that kind of writing, please don't worry. Your writing is a work in progress, and even a few compound or complex sentences will lend a variety to your prose without pushing you dangerously into the Land of the Compound-Complex Sentence. Give yourself time to develop your ear — and your confidence. It will come, especially now that you have a firmer grasp of the basics.

## ROUNDUP

1. Good writing depends on an appreciation for sentences, which are the building blocks of a writer's craft.

2. The eight parts of speech are nouns, pronouns, verbs, adjectives, adverbs, prepositions, conjunctions, and interjections. Words or groups of words that make

up these parts of speech manifest certain consistent behaviors.

3. All sentences must contain a subject and a predicate.

4. A sentence may also contain objects, both direct and indirect.

5. All sentences fall into one of four types: simple, compound, complex, and compound-complex.

6. Sentences go wrong in three main ways: they can be fragments, run-ons, or comma splices. (The comma splice is a variation of the run-on.)

7. Varying your sentence structure is key to good writing.

# Move from Draft to Draft

When I was a young man, still in my twenties, I was turning out short stories one after the other. On the whole, they were pretty good stories, I have to say, even though the *New Yorker* obstinately refused to publish them. One of them came to the attention of a renowned editor named Ted Solotaroff, who had a literary magazine at the time called the *New American Review*. Solotaroff was prepared to publish my story, but then the magazine abruptly folded. (Ouch — but that's a writer's life.)

A few years ago, I came across a quotation from Solotaroff that not only retrieved him from the far recesses of my memory, but also struck me as being very wise:

> Writing a first draft is like groping one's way into a dark room, or overhearing a faint conversation, or telling a joke whose punch line you've forgotten. One writes

mainly to rewrite, for rewriting and revising are how one's mind comes to inhabit the material fully.

Some twenty-five years after that initial intersection with Solotaroff, I wrote a lengthy proposal for a book that was intended to chronicle from scratch my involvement in growing a synagogue. I connected with an agent named Laurie Fox, herself a writer, who was quite taken with my work. When she edited the proposal and returned it to me, however, I was shocked, for the manuscript was littered with changes. *Omigod*, I found myself thinking. *After all these years of turning out book after book, am I really that bad a writer?*

When I began to go over the edits more carefully, however, my initial panic subsided and I realized, with considerable exhilaration, that this was the first time I had ever been edited by somebody so expert. And I realized, better late than never, that there was a lot about writing I could still learn — precision, most of all. The Duchess of Windsor was reputed to have said that one can never be too rich or too thin, and in that same spirit a writer can never be too precise (or too rich). That was the lesson I took away from that particular tutorial. Unfortunately, the book didn't sell — big ouch — but that's a writer's life (or have I said that already?).

Not too long after that episode, my writing career went through another downturn, and out of necessity I found myself transitioning in large part from primarily creative endeavors to business writing. I had mouths to feed, after all. So I became a copywriter, first for the Book-of-the-Month Club, writing capsule descriptions of the videos it sold (I'm a film nut, so that was fun), and then for marketing firms that specialized in creating communications for colleges and universities.

Entering the world of copywriting turned out to be a great thing for me, not just because it provided a good steady income, but also because it helped me become a far more precise writer. I had to be able to hear and reflect what my clients wished to convey, and I had to collaborate with graphic designers, web developers, and account executives, crafting my copy to meet their needs. Over time, I became known as an extremely "clean" writer, one whose work did not require much poring over.

What I am describing here is my evolution as a writer, which has been going on for some forty years. At no point on that time line has the learning ever stopped. Writing is not something you learn once and for all, like the Heimlich maneuver or double-entry bookkeeping. It is something you must work *at*, continually, sometimes with frustration, sometimes with elation, often with both feelings in play simultaneously.

When I help people with their writing, I can see them develop an understanding of writing as a process that is made up of a series of distinct stages — that is, drafts. When they realize that, then they can begin to relax a little and experience the joy of rewriting. In fact, when you let yourself go with the process, you can see how things shape up from draft to draft, which is exciting, satisfying, and, yes, even a bit joyful.

As we navigate this step, I will do my best to convey what takes place (or should take place) from draft to draft. The goal is for you to understand the implications of being in a first or a second or a third draft. Even if you find yourself floundering in your first or second draft, you will be less inclined to panic if you understand that some degree of floundering comes with the territory.

When I work with someone on a short piece — a 500- to 1,000-word essay, a speech, or a letter, for instance — I always tell that person that it might take anywhere from three to seven or eight drafts to get it right. That seven-or-eight number is likely to elicit a significant gulp, but I point out that there is no stigma to having to write more drafts. Finishing a piece in three drafts is not inherently "better" than finishing a piece in eight drafts.

Some pieces are simply more complex and require more work. Your piece might be covering a much wider arc of time, for instance, and time is never easy to handle. The complexity might also have to do with point of view. Should you have written your piece in the present instead of the past tense? Would it have been more effective in third person than first? You will confront many issues when you write, but the work of writing should be an experience of real intellectual vitality, not one of fear and discouragement.

When you start out with a piece of writing, you will inevitably have to get over a number of humps, such as procrastination, which we discussed at length in Step Two. Again, it is important to understand that your progress through a piece of writing becomes much easier when you develop a better understanding of exactly what takes place at the various points in the process. Although the issues addressed certainly carry over from first draft to second draft to third, each draft should have a primary focus that is different from the draft that precedes it and the one that follows. This prevents the feeling of simply treading water — or sinking.

Essentially, writing is about executing your vision. By making cuts, nipping and tucking, rearranging, reimagining, and polishing, you will be molding your vision into its fully executed, fully realized form. That is exciting and challenging work that becomes a little easier when you have a better sense of the overall drafting process.

## Drafting: The Map

In order to develop an overview of the drafting process, try to envision a map that identifies four stops along the way: First Draft, Second Draft, Third Draft, and Polishing and Proofreading. Ultimately, there may be more stops than those, but for right now let's try to keep it simple.

### First Draft

After you've procrastinated — spent time bouncing balls, playing Sudoku, cleaning grout, or whatever — let's assume that you have come up with some semblance of a first draft. At the very least, there is visible text on a page. Even though that may bring some momentary relief, you might soon begin to despair. "Look at that writing," you tell yourself. "It's awful. It's ludicrous." You may just as well curl into a ball and stream Netflix, which is what you really wanted to do in the first place.

Now, now. Pull yourself together. You're simply experiencing those First Draft Blues.

Beginning a project is often a challenge — and soon enough we will discuss the difficulties that can surround *actual* beginnings (i.e., the opening sentences of your piece). At this initial stage, however, you need to sort out your goals.

When you're working on your first draft, what you're really trying to do is to develop a structure. As we've discussed, in writing so many issues are involved and so many decisions need to be made that the writer is often tempted to go down pathways that may seem interesting but that can, in fact, become cul-de-sacs. So once you get your first draft down, you must then cast a jaundiced eye upon your work and be as critical as you know how to be. Let me point out some areas to pay attention to as you make your critique.

## Concept

When you sit down to read your piece, you may find that there is a real problem with the underlying concept. I see that often with my college applicants, who want to dazzle the world with their concepts. "Let me tell this story from the point of view of my dog," they might say. Or, "Wouldn't it be interesting if I turned my whole essay into a dream, so that I would not have to be moored to any kind of reality?" And my response to those ideas is *no* and *no*. Sometimes concepts come across as desperate maneuvers to attract attention or to "dazzle," as these writers aspire to do. As a general rule, go easy on the dazzle. Rein your concepts in, and never let your concept rule the day. Concepts were invented to be torn down.

Crushed as my student writers are when I rain on their conceptual parade, I tell them that there is no point in moaning and groaning about a first draft that has gone conceptually wrong. Such things happen. I always remind writers that when they're dealing with a short piece of writing, they can start over again if necessary. It's not a tragedy. I have written first drafts of novels that have gone conceptually awry, and that is not a tragedy either (but, boy, does it hurt). Ultimately, the only thing you can do with a concept that isn't working is to cut your losses and forge ahead.

### Presentation

Conceptual problems may require that you start all over again, but other kinds of problems do not necessarily require such drastic remedies. For instance, you may have written a piece in which the concept is fine, but the treatment has fallen flat. And why was that? Well, check your language. Is it tight? Is it dull? Is it stilted? Have you been a cliché junkie, gorging on "eager beavers" and "busy bees"?

Issues of tone can also come into play at this stage. Do you sound stuffy, formal, somehow aloof? Or have you been overly confessional to the point that your reader feels as if she is standing two inches from your face and you are completely oblivious to social boundaries?

In our next step, we're going to devote our attention to presentation issues, focusing on matters like metaphors, jargon, and slang. Noisome as those problems can be, the good news is that they are often easy to remedy. Just dump that metaphor and junk that jargon. Your sensitivity to writing issues will develop as you go along, and you will become more attuned to issues of presentation, particularly after you let a piece sit. (Remember that stale constructions become even more noticeably stale after they've sat a bit.)

## Structure

Although flaws in concept and presentation can affect your first draft, faulty structure is usually the culprit and will generally be the focus of your work at this stage.

One reason less experienced writers often have difficulty with structure is that they are overly attached to a strictly linear approach. This is not surprising when you stop to think about it. When we don't know where we're going, we tend to proceed in a cautious manner, convinced that if we follow a straight line, we will arrive at our destination. That might make sense for getting from Philadelphia to Pittsburgh, but the truth is that writing is a more open-ended kind of journey.

It is therefore important to understand that structure is a highly flexible thing. A good piece of writing does not necessarily have its beginning, middle, and end *in that order*. Your current end might be much more effective when placed at the beginning, so that the rest of the piece leads up to it, for instance. In the same vein, your current middle could well become your new beginning. Often when I work with a writer, we discover that the first couple of paragraphs that are slowing down the first draft are essentially what Hollywood screenwriters refer to as "backstory" — the history or background of a character that is important for the writer to know but that doesn't necessarily make its way onto the screen.

Typically, these unnecessary beginnings are full of extraneous information. "It was a sunny Tuesday afternoon in

April as I headed down to Market Square. I always loved visiting that part of town, with its quaint shops and trendy cafés, but that day I had something else on my mind." Such information might be important for the writer to know, but not the reader, and my writers are surprised to see that they can simply lop off such paragraphs altogether. In short, whether you are writing a personal narrative or a letter of complaint, the same principle applies: look at the structure of your first draft to see if you actually need all that you've written.

As you proceed with the critical reading of your first draft, which I always suggest be done aloud, as the ear picks up issues that often escape the eye, you'll begin to see and hear structural problems. Does it feel as though it is taking too long to get into the piece? Is the middle section bloated and baggy? Is the ending abrupt? Would the ending work better if you shifted it to the beginning and worked backward?

As you engage in this kind of critical reading, you'll do so with the understanding that proportion is an important piece of the structural picture. Think of an outfit in which the jacket is too short and the pants are too long. In it, you look like you should be driving a very tiny car around a circus ring. There should be a reasonably proportional relationship between your opening, midsection, and ending. If not, fix it.

Do what you can to build a strong structure in the first draft — but also keep in mind that your structure can still change in your second, third, or even fourth draft. In fact, your structure can always change if it has to. When it's right, you will know it. It will feel solid and elegant.

## Second Draft

By the time you get to your second draft, your structure may be largely in place (or not; as we've said, structural issues can linger way beyond your first draft), but things may still not be working as they should.

One problem could be that you haven't identified the conflict in your piece. If you think back to Step Three, you will remember our discussion of storytelling and how a solid understanding of the elements of a narrative can infuse so much of what you write, from personal essays, to wedding toasts, to eulogies, to letters of complaint, to letters of recommendation, and more. A good part of what people write about and have always written about is conflict and how we resolve it. Until that conflict makes itself known in your piece — to the reader, yes, but, most important, to you, the writer — you will likely be ambling along in a kind of discursive and desultory way.

Frank was a lawyer whose daughter, Lauren, was getting married. As father of the bride, he was charged with writing a wedding toast. He decided to play out the concept of the legal contract between bride and groom, hoping that the cleverness of his concept would carry the day. In fact, his concept wasn't that clever to start out with and, even worse, it was written in language that people don't want to hear. So a new concept had to be put in place in order for the content to emerge — content that was closely connected to conflict.

Now what kind of conflict might this father of the bride be exploring? Some possibilities:

The arrival of a "stranger" who is joining the family.

The challenges of arranging a wedding.

The passage of time.

Frank's concern that he and his wife might not have set a good enough example of married life for their daughter.

The reality that Lauren won't need Daddy the way she used to.

Many choices and directions await that father of the bride, but the important point to understand here is that the concept must serve the content/conflict. The people seated under that tent want to hear about the very issues that they themselves have faced or may one day face. They are looking for insights, tenderness, and warmth. Cleverness palls after a moment or two; content, if it's good, will keep on giving. In other words, good content paired with a good concept will carry the day.

When I work with a writer and we go over a first draft that has fallen short of its mark, I will often ask the question: "What is this piece about?" You would be surprised how hard it can be to answer something that simple and direct. Maybe because it's not so simple? We often get ahead of ourselves when we write, hoping that clever notions, flashy images, and fancy words are going to do the job, but that stuff is essentially window dressing. First, you need the window: into ourselves and onto the world, offering insight into how people live.

So as we toil in the trenches of the Second Draft, we

must ask ourselves that question directly: "What is this piece about?" If you are writing a letter of complaint to a customer-service representative regarding the awful night you spent at the Last Resort, it's not enough to just bellyache. You don't want to spend four paragraphs detailing the water spots on the ceiling, the dingy towels in the bathroom, the suspicious hair on the pillow, and the bug on the carpet and then wait until your last paragraph to ask for whatever it is that you have set out to get. And that is the point of this letter: to resolve an issue and come away with something like a refund or a credit.

To recap, you want to structure your piece, whether it's a personal essay, a letter of complaint, a wedding toast, a eulogy, a letter to the editor, a book review, or something else altogether, so that your structure supports your content, which will often connect to some kind of conflict.

In the First Draft stage, the structural solutions can be quite straightforward. A writer might say, "Ah, I see that there isn't time to start this toast with Lauren's birth. I think I'll lop off the first three paragraphs and start closer to the time she met Armando." By the Second Draft stage, however, the writer might want to be a little more adventurous with the structure. "I think I'll try starting this with Lauren's telling me and her mother that she met the man of her dreams. Then I'll go back in time to when she was little and *I* was the man of her dreams. Then I'll work my way up to the present, talking about how she and I always had a strong bond and loved to ski, cook, and watch old movies together. And then I'll take it to when I met Armando for the first time and realized that he was absolutely the right guy for my daughter."

When a writer asks me if I think a certain section would go better here than there, I usually say, "Try it. It's your piece. Follow your instinct. See how it feels. And if it's not right, no big deal. Try something else." I want people to understand that writing offers a great deal of flexibility. Take this section and put it there. Take that section and stick it here. See what happens.

Today's technology, featuring the ability to cut and paste, makes the rewriting process vastly easier than it used to be. As much as I hate to admit it, I am old enough to remember when rewriting required actual cutting and pasting with scissors and an Elmer's glue stick, and that wasn't any fun. The fear of making mistakes, so prevalent among those who do not view themselves as writers, inhibits the very sense of freedom and creativity that is crucial to good writing. So don't be inhibited. Use your cut-and-paste function freely and productively.

### Third Draft

Our goal in the Third Draft stage is to get grounded in what happens from draft to draft. Please do not regard these drafts as set in stone. Nothing could be farther from the truth. Certain issues that you might expect to come into play in your first draft might actually not surface until the third draft, while issues that usually show themselves in the third draft might somehow surface in your first draft. What I am trying to do here is to give you a *general* sense of the flow of the drafts.

To recap, the First Draft has you reviewing your piece in

a sort of global way, checking for the merits of its concept, for the quality of its presentation, and almost inevitably for major flaws in structure. In the Second Draft, you will be playing once more with structure, specifically with the way in which it supports your content. Now, at the Third Draft stage, the structure might be looking good and the conflict is clear, but something is still missing. Could it be The Point?

Think back now, if you will, to Step Three, when we were discussing the elements of a narrative and we identified The Point, which was the very reason you were writing your piece in the first place. There is no benefit in piling on conflict (the water stains on the ceiling of that subpar motel, the dingy towels in the bathroom, and the flattened beetle on the carpet) if that conflict doesn't lead to The Point. So what exactly is The Point of your letter of complaint? It could be any (or close to all) of the following:

> You don't deserve to run a motel, and I am reporting you to the Board of Health.
>
> You don't deserve to run a motel, and I am going to savage you on Trip Advisor.
>
> You haven't run your motel well, so I am entitled to a refund.
>
> I have stayed at Last Resort before with much pleasure, but this time you obviously had an off night. Kindly credit me, and I may return someday.

All of the above could be perfectly reasonable Points, but it is important that you know exactly what your letter is asking for. What are you looking to get out of this letter? What do you want your reader to get out of it? Although more experienced writers may go into a piece of writing armed from the very beginning with a clear sense of The Point, less experienced writers usually rely on drafts to uncover The Point — and then may need to make additional adjustments draft to draft to ensure that The Point is supported by the structure and tone.

Ah, tone. That's a big part of what you will be scrutinizing in your Third Draft. Later in the book we will focus on issues of tone, but for now let's just say that you will be paying close attention to your voice. In fact, this may be the first time in your life that you have ever really thought about the quality of your voice, at least in the sense of how it is manifested in your writing. Are you dry? Stuffy? Flippant? Sentimental? Overly intense? Tone can go wrong in many ways, and we'll be looking at issues that influence tone, such as word choice, jargon, clichés, and metaphors.

## Polishing and Proofreading

As you know, you could well be facing more than three drafts to get your piece right. Remember Ernest Hemingway, whose style we were discussing in the last step? Hemingway was reputed to have written the last page of *A Farewell to Arms* thirty-seven times. So if you have to rewrite your toast for your daughter's special day six times, what's the big deal? The fact of the matter is that more structural work, more tonal work, and more pinpointing of The Point may need to take place. At some point, however, your structural work will have fallen into place, The Point will be apparent and strong, and you can focus your efforts primarily on the polishing that needs to take place.

No matter what we are writing, we must always strive to make it as good as it can be. Obviously, that is not to say that everything we write is pointed toward posterity. Our letter of complaint is not going to be preserved in the Library of Congress, after all. Even so, we should always seek to attain a level of excellence. A serious lapse of grammar in a cover letter, for instance, can mean the difference between getting an interview and not getting one. Although that may be exactly what nervous writers don't want to hear, it is important to know that there are proven ways to make our work cleaner and significantly freer of errors.

In the final stage of the writing process, we bring polishing to the next level through proofreading. Let me just say that not everyone is a born proofreader or copyeditor. Those functions are best performed by people who possess a certain kind of God-given ability and mindset. Such individuals can catch inconsistencies, for instance, that 99 percent of the rest of us would be completely unaware of. Unless you are a professional writer in whose work a publisher is investing, however, you will not have a copyeditor or proofreader at your disposal.

So then, for most of us, proofreading will be a hit-and-miss process, but it can still be enhanced by a number of useful techniques and strategies. We will go into the nitty-gritty of those proofreading techniques when we get to Step Seven, but for now just note that proofreading represents the end stage of the process, in which your goal is to produce as clean a piece of writing as possible. When you've managed to do that, then your work will be finished.

## Paragraphs

Now that we have gained an overview of the writing process and can better understand what takes place at the various intervals in that process, we are going to look at a few other issues that have considerable bearing on the structure of a piece. Let's start with paragraphs.

I often see writing that demonstrates very little understanding of paragraph structure, which is a shame, because paragraphs serve an important purpose. They are something of a mystery to many, however, in part because there is no set rule for when to introduce a new paragraph. Some might say that you should form a new paragraph to introduce a new idea. That's true — but then some paragraphs build upon existing ideas, so newness is not the only rationale for introducing a paragraph.

One might more accurately say that the best reason for introducing a new paragraph is to refresh your reader. This makes sense when you consider the contract between reader and writer. Think of the relief you yourself experience as a reader when one paragraph ends and you can get a bit of breathing space before a new paragraph begins. Chapters offer the same kind of relief — but you don't have to worry about chapters yet. The scope of your writing right now is probably not that ambitious.

So what should paragraphs look like? Should they be long? Should they be short? Can you have both long *and* short paragraphs? Sure. They can be any or all of the above.

In large part, good paragraph structure is determined by an innate sense of rhythm that should develop generally in your writing as well as by the specific rhythm that is appropriate to the piece you are working on. An action piece — let's say, a column describing a basketball game — will tend to have shorter paragraphs. A "think" piece — an editorial or an academic paper — will tend to have longer paragraphs. (Of course, there are powerful exceptions to those rules.)

Determining the length of a paragraph is really a matter of intuition. Paragraphs that feel too long *are* too long. Paragraphs that are too short may feel choppy (or they may feel just right). Is it okay to have a paragraph that is only one sentence? Some people say no, but the answer is yes. A one-sentence paragraph is completely kosher — but too many one-sentence paragraphs will most likely feel choppy.

It is best to vary the lengths of your paragraphs. One long, two short. One short, two long — that sort of thing. Just as we discussed in Step Four when we were exploring the need to vary sentence lengths, here too variation is desirable.

Paragraph structure can be quite flexible. My students and I often find that we can take the last sentence of one paragraph and make it the first sentence of the next paragraph — or vice versa. In so doing, we've altered the sense of what we've written as well as the rhythm, and we've improved the flow of the piece.

Now let's touch on the difficult subjects of beginnings and endings.

## In the Beginning

Consider these opening lines from several novels:

All happy families are alike; each unhappy family is unhappy in its own way.

It is a truth universally acknowledged, that a single man in possession of a good fortune, must be in want of a wife.

Lolita, light of my life, fire of my loins.

What writer wouldn't kill to come up with an opening line as good as those, from *Anna Karenina*, *Pride and Prejudice*, and *Lolita*, respectively? There is no substitute for a good beginning — and until you have one, there is no better reason for tearing out your hair. Beginnings and endings always seem to be the hardest parts of any piece.

As previously mentioned, I often counsel writers to lop off their first couple of paragraphs altogether. Sometimes you can start, as I indicated above, right in the middle of things (*in media res*), plunging the reader into the action:

Joanne burst into tears.

The tire blew.

"If I hear that one more time, I'll explode!"

Openings such as these, even when they run the risk of being a tad corny, are meant to grab your attention. They are far superior to other kinds of openings I often see, which sound like these:

Where to begin? Ah, that's the question.

I treasure art above almost everything, which is why what happened in the museum that day was so memorable.

"The family is one of life's masterpieces," said George Santayana.

If you look at those three openings, you'll see the kinds of problems that can befall the less experienced writer. The first opening is completely irrelevant. Sorting out where to begin is your job, not your reader's. The second is dull, feels padded, and, like the first, is irrelevant. Why not just tell us what happened in the museum that day? Don't tell us what you're going to tell us.

The third type of opening is becoming increasingly prevalent and can be blamed on the internet, which encourages googling around for quotations, often from sources you've never heard of. For some reason, George Santayana, a Spanish-born twentieth-century essayist, novelist, and philosopher, always seems to come up. He is little remembered today for any significant works, but apparently he was partial to aphorisms, which explains why he's all over sites like BrainyQuote, Quote Garden, and such.

I suggest that writers leave this Toastmasters approach behind. Readers — who are people just like yourself — enjoy knowing how others deal with real-life situations. So keep it real. And keep in mind that you may need to rework your beginnings many times over. That just comes with the job of writing.

## And So It Ends

Beginnings are so hard to get right because the writer is still finding his or her way through the material, but endings can also trip up the less experienced and insecure writer who just wants to exit a piece as quickly as possible. That's why I see silly endings like these:

> Boy, did I learn my lesson.
>
> I vowed to do better next time.
>
> I thought to myself, "If only I had to do it all over again."

These are not good endings. In fact, they're tags. A tag can best be described as a sort of cute little construction (well, at least the writer thinks it's cute) that is meant to wrap things up neatly. Generally, they don't work and should be left off.

Another kind of flawed ending is the one I refer to as a "fade." The writer has no idea how to end things and so relies on this sort of sentence:

> This was a day that shall linger in my memory for as long as I live.

Yawn.

Remember, one of the foremost rules of writing is: "Don't tell it. Show it." If you can *show* me why this thing that you chose to write about is so memorable, you don't have to *tell* me at the end that it was memorable.

The "fade" becomes even more awkward when the unsure writer piles on qualifiers. In such situations, you get constructions that sound like this:

> This was a day that will really linger in my memory, probably for as long as I live.

The reliance on qualifiers like *really*, *probably*, *kind of*, and *sort of* is a dead giveaway that the writer does not have a firm grip on the wheel. It signals an insecurity that makes readers, in turn, nervous. And readers don't like to be nervous. They long to be held securely in the hands of a writer who is in command.

It takes a confident writer to resist filling in all the blanks at the end. The less confident writer is more likely to veer in the direction of the Aesop's fables model, providing a moral that neatly sums things up. By not filling in all the blanks, writers show that they respect the fact that readers have an active role in this process and may wish to fill in a few of the blanks themselves.

Endings also emerge more clearly and effectively when writers understand The Point of what they have set out to write. Having a clear idea of what drew you to your material in the first place and understanding where your thinking has led you will help you clarify where you want to leave your readers. They need to understand The Point just as much as you do.

Given the difficulty in crafting strong endings, how will you know if you have succeeded? Probably the best indicator will be the responses of your readers. If you get quizzical looks or wan smiles when readers finish your piece, then you know there is a problem, and that problem could well be your ending. Not to panic, however. Just go back to work and come up with a new ending — or several new endings. May the best ending win.

And again, the same goes for your beginnings. And don't forget to read it all out loud. When you read your work out loud, you can often hear what's good and what isn't. If you read it out loud and it all sounds good to your ears, then chances are it *is* good. And don't stop until you feel confident that you got it just right.

## Up Close

For our Up Close exercise, let's return to the wedding toast of our friend Frank. As you recall, Frank started out wanting to put a clever spin on things by concocting his toast in legalese. After a few unenthusiastic readings, however, he acknowledged that the *concept* of his toast was at fault. Part of the problem was that Frank's toast put *him* ahead of everyone and everything else. In fact, no one at the wedding really cared that Frank was an attorney or was interested in his parody of legal language. They were much more interested in hearing his honest thoughts and feelings about his daughter and son-in-law on their special day.

Like most people asked to give a toast, however, Frank felt it was incumbent upon him to somehow be clever instead of straightforward, so he tried other gimmicky approaches for his second draft. He borrowed David Letterman's Top Ten format and did a draft of the "Top Ten Reasons Why Lauren and Armando Should Be Married":

10. Because they both play to win.
9. Because they've both seen *Mamma Mia!* more than three times.
8. Because they both love Brussels sprouts.

And so it went. When he tried this out on his wife, however, she merely smiled wanly. Frank came to understand that, just as David Letterman had retired, so too should the Top Ten format be given a rest. Again, this was a *concept* problem. Frank had glommed onto a concept, which, unfortunately, also happened to be a stale one, and this robbed him of the opportunity to speak from the heart, which is what this situation required.

The message that guided Frank in his third draft was, in fact, to do just that: speak from the heart. When he stopped to consider what was so special about his daughter, he remembered a time when the two of them were driving along a country road and she made him stop to help a turtle cross the road, so it wouldn't get hit by a car. The fact that it turned out to be a snapping turtle added some of that juicy stuff called conflict to his toast, and this is what his third draft looked like:

> As the father of the bride, I knew that I would be called upon today to make a toast. What is it that I really wanted to say about Lauren? I asked myself. She was a complicated person. How could I do her justice in just a few words?
>
> Should I talk about her determination? Her daring? Her loyalty? Yes, all of those attributes should be addressed. But I didn't want to miss the part of her that has always been particularly special to me and her mother: her kindness.
>
> I think back to a time about three years ago when I happened to be driving down some back road with her. We were chatting about this and that when suddenly, up ahead, we saw some large black object.

"Stop!" she cried, and I screeched to a halt.

There was a turtle. Before I could say another word, she jumped out of the car. I knew what an animal lover she was — but I also knew that Good Samaritans can get killed in a roadside rescue. I jumped out too, and when we got closer, we saw that it was not just any turtle but the sizable snapping variety.

I turned to go, but Lauren grabbed me by the arm. "Dad," she said, "we've got to help."

"No way," I replied. "They bite."

"Don't be a wuss," she said, as she walked over to a ditch and found a four-foot piece of tree limb that she could use to poke the creature. And poke she did, until it was on the other side of the road and out of harm's way.

Whether it's on the soccer field or in a debate or now, on her job, Lauren is not to be messed with. At the same time, she is loved by all, because her determination is underlaid by a real sense of kindness. Armando, you're the right man for her. You've got the determination, you've got the kindness, you're no wussy boy, and you know when to get out of her way.

Let's lift a glass to Lauren and Armando. May they have a long life of happiness together, free of snapping turtles.

We can see here that as soon as Frank dropped the cleverness — that is, the conceptual problems that were leading him into that legalese gambit and that David Letterman Top Ten approach — he was able to make room for some honest emotion, which is exactly what people come to weddings to hear. And once he was clear that he wanted to tell a warm personal story, he was able to focus on matters of structure and presentation.

There was still work to be done, however. After getting some readings of his third draft, Frank realized that he could do away with his opening two paragraphs:

> As the father of the bride, I knew that I would be called upon today to make a toast. What is it that I really wanted to say about Lauren? I asked myself. She was a complicated person. How could I do her justice in just a few words?
>
> Should I talk about her determination? Her daring? Her loyalty? Yes, all of those attributes should be addressed. But I didn't want to miss the part of her that has always been particularly special to me and her mother: her kindness.

That was background or, more accurately, out-loud thinking that was useful for preparing to write this story, but not anything that his readers or listeners needed to know.

He also felt that his writing could benefit from a little more pizzazz, so he looked for more original and interesting ways to express himself throughout. This is what his fourth draft looked like:

> About three years ago, Lauren and I were driving down a back road on the way to doing some kind of errand. I think, if I recall correctly, we were going to pick up a futon for her new apartment. We were cruising along, listening to Van Morrison, the sun was shining, and it was a nice way to be spending a father-daughter

Saturday morning. And then, suddenly, something big and black loomed ahead on the road. Was it a trash bag? A car part? As we got closer, we could see that it was no trash bag and no car part. It was a turtle.

"Stop!" Lauren cried, and I screeched to a halt.

Animal lover that she is, she jumped out of the car and raced toward the creature. I followed, doing my best to keep up with her. As we approached, we could see that it was not just any turtle but a whopping big snapper.

"Come on, Lauren," I said. "Let's go."

"No way," she replied. "We've got to help — "

"But they bite."

"Don't be a wuss, Dad," she said, as she walked over to a ditch and found a four-foot piece of tree limb that she could use to poke the creature. And poke she did, until it was on the other side of the road and out of harm's way.

As most of you know, when Lauren gets an idea in her head, she usually sees it through. Whether it's on the soccer field or in a debate or on a deserted country road steering a snapping turtle, Lauren is not to be messed with. This may explain why she has become a litigator, like dear old Dad. But tough as she may be, that toughness and determination is underlaid by a sense of kindness that is always with her and always authentic. There isn't much that scares her, and there isn't much that deters her, but there is a great deal that she cares about deeply.

Armando, I don't know how you feel about snapping turtles, but I'm convinced that you're the right man for Lauren. You've got the same kind of determination as she does and the same kind of kindness. You know how to get out of her way when you need to, but Lord knows you're no wuss. The two of you together are going to really be something.

Please join me in lifting a glass to Lauren and Armando. May they have a long life of happiness together, free of snapping turtles, if possible, but filled with purpose, always kindness, and love.

Among the changes that brought Frank's effort to a higher level were the following:

1. He gave more flavor to that Saturday morning drive ("We were cruising along, listening to Van Morrison, the sun was shining...").
2. He pored over the text to amp up the language wherever he could. (For instance, he changed "the sizable snapping variety," which sounded rather dry and stuffy, to "a whopping big snapper." More fun.)
3. He brought dialogue into the piece in a more dynamic way. (In the pages ahead, we will be discussing dialogue — a useful device for your toolbox.)
4. Also, as the structure became more solid, Frank's ability to articulate the emotional truths of the toast came through. Because he felt more supported by the structure of the piece, he was freed up to focus on expression.
5. You might also have noticed that he dropped the

reference to Good Samaritans getting killed. A bit grim for a wedding toast, no?

6. He changed the description of what Armando was not, a "wussy boy," to "wuss." "Wussy boy" sounds homophobic, and we must always check out our writing to make sure it is free of racial, gender, and sexual stereotypes. *Wuss* is not a pleasant word — Merriam-Webster defines it as a "weak, cowardly, or ineffectual person" — and Frank might have left that reference out altogether. At the very least, however, *wuss* wouldn't cause anyone to stand up and walk out of the room.

In his fifth draft, Frank played around with the structure some more:

"Stop!"

About three years ago, Lauren and I were driving down a back road on the way to doing some kind of errand. I think, if I recall correctly, we were going to pick up a futon for her new apartment. We were cruising along, listening to Van Morrison, the sun was shining, and it was a nice way to be spending a father-daughter Saturday morning. And then, suddenly, something big and black loomed ahead on the road. Was it a trash bag? A car part? As we got closer, we could see that it was no trash bag and no car part. It was a turtle.

"Stop!" Lauren cried, and I screeched to a halt.

Animal lover that she is, she jumped out of the car and raced toward the creature. I followed, doing my best to keep up with her. As we approached, we could see that it was not just any turtle, but a whopping big snapper.

"Come on, Lauren," I said. "Let's go."

"No way," she replied. "We've got to help — "

"But they bite."

"Don't be a wuss, Dad," she said, as she walked over to a ditch and found a four-foot piece of tree limb that she could use to poke the creature. And poke she did, until it was on the other side of the road and out of harm's way.

As most of you know, when Lauren gets an idea in her head, she usually sees it through. Whether it's on the soccer field or in a debate or on a deserted country road steering a snapping turtle, Lauren is not to be messed with. This may explain why she has become a litigator, like dear old Dad. But tough as she may be, that toughness and determination is underlaid by a sense of kindness that is always with her and always authentic. There isn't much that scares her, and there isn't much that deters her, and there is a great deal that she cares about deeply.

Armando, I don't know how you feel about snapping turtles, but I'm convinced that you're the right man for Lauren. You've got the same kind of determination as she does and the same kind of kindness. You know how to get out of her way when you need to, but Lord knows you're no wuss. The two of you together are going to really be something.

Please join me in lifting a glass to Lauren and Armando. May they have a long life of happiness together, free of snapping turtles, if possible, but filled with purpose, always kindness, and love.

In this version, the toast starts *in media res* — "Stop!" — which can certainly be an effective way to capture the attention of a roomful of people who have been sipping potent potables. Frank got so into the writing that he even committed to a few more drafts, focusing on word choice, tonal issues, and general all-around polishing. What he ultimately came up with might not win the Pulitzer Prize for wedding toasts, but it certainly put a smile on the lips of all who were there and made the room feel warmer, more intimate, and more connected, which is exactly what a wedding toast should do.

Good job, Frank. You followed the writing process from draft to draft, and you came away with exactly what you and your audience were looking for.

## ROUNDUP

1. Writing is a process that is made up of stages (drafts), each with identifiable goals.
2. When it comes to writing, there is no set number of drafts that you can plan on, nor is there any stigma to having to write more drafts.
3. The First Draft generally focuses on structural issues, though issues related to concept and presentation must also be scrutinized.
4. A purely linear structure is not necessarily a writer's best choice.

5. More structural work commonly takes place during the Second Draft stage.

6. By the time you reach your Third Draft, you should be asking yourself: What is this piece about? That is, what is The Point of this piece?

7. We must always strive for excellence in our writing, and so Polishing and Proofreading is a critical stage in the process.

8. Paragraphs play a big role in shaping structure.

9. Paragraphs can introduce new ideas, but, most important, they are designed to refresh the reader.

10. Beginnings and endings are often the hardest parts to get right.

# Watch Your Tone

"Hey, homies. Whatcha all think of a chapter 'bout tone? You like da sound of dem apples? If so, please indicate your preference accordingly, and we will do our best to serve you."

There, in 33 words, you have a mash-up that shows just how wrong even a small piece of writing can go when the writer does not keep a firm hand on the tone rudder. The first 17 words comprise a scatological glop of homeboy slang, while the final 16 words convey the aura of anonymity that can render form letters so deadly. In other words, the reader is getting the worst of it from either end.

Many writers suffer an identity crisis when it comes to tone. They don't know how they are supposed to sound, or if they wish to sound a certain way, they don't know how to achieve that tone. Consequently, they waffle from one tone to another or get bogged down in one tone altogether, ultimately sounding too informal, too formal, too brash, too fussy, or what have you. In short, these writers don't hear their voice, so they have a hard time making their voice heard.

One of your primary goals as a writer is to capture your *authentic voice*. If you think back to our discussion of sentence structure in Step Four, you will recall the passages we included from Ernest Hemingway and Henry James. The authentic voices of those two writers could not have been more dissimilar. Hemingway's voice was spare and unadorned, with language that was concise to the point of terseness. He also made use of the "unsaid" — that is, the room around the text — and what was not said was often as significant as what was said. In contrast, James's authentic voice was dauntingly complex, even convoluted, and strongly reliant on symbolic imagery. Some readers are more drawn to James's language, some to Hemingway's. Many readers appreciate the unique characteristics of both.

How about you? Do you have an authentic voice?

Chances are, many of you have never considered this question before. We all have a sense of our physiognomy. We can tell you that our nose is aquiline or pug, that our neck is long or short, that our lips are thin or full. We can probably tell you something about our personality as well. We are introverted or extroverted. We are down-to-earth or flighty, calm or nervous, optimistic or pessimistic. But when was the last time you tried to characterize your authentic voice?

Well, there is no time like the present. I invite you to go ahead and try to gauge the nature of your authentic voice.

## How Do I Sound?

It may be easier to approach this subject if I ask you to think about one of your friends and describe how that person sounds to you. You might say "funny" or "wise," "irreverent" or "serious," or "modest" or "cynical." You can hear that person's voice in your head, and you recognize that the way that person sounds is probably a big piece of why the two of you are friends.

You sound a certain way to others as well. Just as you have a thumbprint, so too do you have an authentic voice that people conjure up when they think of you. Now, the goal is for you to think about your voice and how it sounds to others. A good way to begin is by considering the following list of descriptors and choosing any that fit you:

| | | |
|---|---|---|
| Accessible | Confident | Organized |
| Aloof | Cute | Outspoken |
| Amiable | Dry | Reserved |
| Apologetic | Earthy | Sarcastic |
| Arrogant | Emotional | Serious |
| Authoritative | Gentle | Steady |
| Bold | Impulsive | Stubborn |
| Brash | Irreverent | Unflappable |
| Caring | Logical | Whimsical |
| Casual | Methodical | Witty |
| Cerebral | Modest | Wry |

Well, that's certainly a lot of words, and there are many more to choose from. Please note too that more than one of these descriptors can characterize your authentic voice. "Confident" and "cerebral" with a bit of "outspoken" thrown in? "Casual" and "unflappable" with a touch of "whimsical"? Why not?

You don't have to restrict yourself to self-testing either. Ask friends and family to help gauge your authentic voice. Ask them: "How do I sound to you? Can you put a label on the qualities that make me who I am?" Show them the list of descriptors and ask them to assign one or more to you.

If you wind up assigning yourself (or you are assigned by others) any descriptors that don't make you feel especially good about yourself, like "arrogant" or "brash" or "aloof," you can begin to consciously mitigate those qualities as you continue to develop your authentic voice. Arrogance is not a widely appreciated quality, so you may want to dial it down so you come across as "confident" or "bold" instead. Similarly, if "sarcastic" comes to mind when you're describing yourself or others are describing you, you should know that such a tone is not going to ingratiate you with most people — or most readers. A little sarcasm is permissible, but a little goes a long way. Again, you'll want to adjust the dial so that your sarcasm plays more as irreverence or wit. The qualities that characterize your authentic voice, whatever those might be, can still be in place, but it is within your power to control them.

When you start to develop a sense of your voice, then you can start to write with greater confidence. You can *hear* your voice, and your ability to do so will help you anchor yourself in most writing situations. You will locate a kind of "sweet spot" in which you will feel comfortable and relaxed and better able to connect with your readers.

I can tell you that I very much hear my authentic voice

when I sit down to write. It is a voice that has served me well. Many readers have told me that they have particularly enjoyed my books, especially those on writing, not simply because they contain valuable information and insights, but also because my tone makes it easier for them to absorb the information. These readers tell me that my tone is conversational, warm, friendly, humorous, informal, relaxed, and highly accessible. And that's nice to hear.

I haven't always had this voice — at least not to this extent. In finding my way as a writer over the course of my career, I have tried on other voices (or at the very least felt compelled to try on other voices as dictated by the assignments I was given). For instance, as I said earlier in this book, I have worked steadily over the years in the world of higher-education marketing, writing materials for colleges and universities. Sometimes those materials are focused on student recruitment, so I write the big glossy brochures, known as "viewbooks," that potential applicants pick up on their campus visits. I also write development materials that are aimed at alumni/ae, soliciting gifts toward new construction or academic programs.

When I write recruitment materials, I keep my audience of sixteen- and seventeen-year-olds firmly in mind. They are many, many years younger than I am, and I neither know nor pretend to know their parlance. (I do know, however, that they would never use the word *parlance*.) Even so, I speak to them respectfully and always with the conviction that we can find common ground despite our age difference. On the other hand, when I write development materials, I envision wealthy alums sitting in leather chairs in a paneled library, and I adjust my voice accordingly. For them, I might well use the word *parlance*.

Interestingly, however, my *authentic voice* does not change from one audience to the other. The colleges that I work for tend to marvel at my ability to strike a conversational chord, both with these young people and with the donors. They note that I never pander or grovel by trying to use language that I'm not comfortable with, but that I make connections by using language that I *am* comfortable with. Feeling comfortable with your writing vastly improves your ability to connect with your readers.

Let me give you an example of what I'm talking about. When I write for wealthy alums sitting in leather chairs, I don't go with the tone usually reserved for that audience in development materials from colleges and universities — stuffy, formal, and filled with nonprofit jargon. (I will discuss jargon later in this section.) The writers of those materials don't visualize their readers, but rather try to get through the "list" of points they feel must be put out there. My success in writing to this audience is that I visualize those readers as human beings, and I draw on my authentic voice, warm and conversational, to make a connection. I don't rely on slang or "language of the day" (also to be discussed) to make my authentic voice conversational. I rely on my capacity for empathy to make an emotional connection, "hearing" those I am writing for and "listening" to them.

You needn't have a conversational tone, as I do, to have an effective authentic voice. Although it's true that most people like a conversational tone, they appreciate other kinds of voices as well. A "dignified" authentic voice could be absolutely fine — so long as it's not a "stuffy" authentic voice. An "authoritative" voice could be much welcomed — so long as it's not a "rigid" voice. An "elegant" voice might make a reader's day — so long as it's not a "pretentious" voice. You should continue to gauge the qualities of your authentic voice and refine them as you can, to get the voice that you feel most comfortable with and that you believe will best connect you to your readers. As you begin to "hear" yourself, you will gain confidence, and eventually others will hear you too.

## Formal vs. Informal

The process of assessing your authentic voice is an ongoing one. Throughout that process, you can adjust your voice by examining a central binary in writing: formal vs. informal.

There are certainly times when it makes sense to be informal, as when we are emailing a friend or leaving a note for the babysitter, and then there are times when we want to assume a more formal tone, as when we are writing to our child's school principal or requesting a refund for a defective product. The problem is that many writers lack the confidence or the ability to stay with a given tone, so their tone wanders within a piece of writing, undercutting its merits significantly.

A general rule of thumb that can be helpful here is to try to stay somewhere in the middle. So, then, if you are writing a letter to the school principal, you do not begin this way:

Dear Mr. Richardson,
Hey! How are you doing? Haven't seen you since Arbor Day. Boy, we planted plenty of trees that day.

Now let me ask you about my Tommy. I don't know what's up, but his teacher has contacted me with some complaints...

Unless you and Mr. Richardson grew up together and shared a bench in the Little League dugout (in which case your salutation would not be "Mr. Richardson"), the tone here is altogether too informal. In certain circumstances, too much informality suggests too much familiarity — and familiarity that is not legitimately claimed can make the recipient (i.e., Mr. Richardson) feel distinctly uncomfortable, as if you are making assumptions about your connection that have no basis and that could even suggest to Mr. Richardson a potential conflict of interest.

At the same time, you do know Mr. Richardson reasonably well. You have spoken to him at school events and even when you've run into him in the produce department of the local supermarket. He lives in the community after all and is a pleasant and approachable person. So, then, this kind of tone would be equally problematic:

Dear Mr. Richardson,
I am writing with concerns about recent occurrences in my son Tommy's classroom. I trust that I have your permission to raise this matter with you and trust as well that this will be kept entirely confidential. It is important to me that I can count on your cooperation.

Since you and Mr. Richardson have been squeezing cantaloupes side by side at FoodLand, there is no need to assume such an impersonal and formal tone. Such a tone will not ingratiate you with a reader, and one might imagine that you are looking to call upon the principal's goodwill in this situation.

What, then, is the answer? You need to find that middle ground, somewhere between formal and informal, that will sound right to your reader's ear. Consider this version:

> Dear Mr. Richardson,
> Recently, something came up in my son Tommy's classroom, and I would like to discuss this matter with you. Tommy's teacher, Mrs. Walker, contacted me last week with serious complaints about his behavior, and I feel that it is necessary to further explore what went on...

That is a calm, measured, reasonable, and even likable approach. It would be received either neutrally or somewhat positively by its recipient — which is exactly how you want such a note to be received. In other words, you want to make sure that, before you get to your "ask" in such a letter, you haven't in any way turned off your reader. And the best way to do that is to walk the line between formal and informal.

## Striking the Balance

How, then, does one find the middle ground between formal and informal? In fact, it is relatively easy to prune away writing that is overly informal. Usually, that problem is rooted less in sentence-structure issues than in content. Look again at that piece of text I showed you above:

> Dear Mr. Richardson,
> Hey! How are you doing? Haven't seen you since

Arbor Day. Boy, we planted plenty of trees that day. Now let me ask you about my Tommy. I don't know what's up, but his teacher has contacted me with some complaints...

The hallmarks of informal style abound in that short space. These include the use of interjections and imperatives (We see "Hey!" but "Wait!" or "Come on!" or "No way!" might also surface). Notice too the use of contractions ("haven't," "don't," "what's"). Contractions are not bad English, but if you are trying to walk the line between formal and informal, you should realize that an all-contractions approach moves the meter significantly toward informal, whereas the total absence of contractions will make your work sound quite formal.

The use of colloquial words and expressions will also move you in the direction of informality. "Plenty of trees" has a distinctly colloquial feeling (as compared with "many trees" or "a large number of trees"). The entire expression "I don't know what's up" is heavily colloquial.

Clichés, which we will discuss as we move along in this step, can also add to that colloquial feeling. Clichés are not in evidence in the text above, but let's reimagine it with a few thrown in (clichés in bold):

Dear Mr. Richardson,
Hey! How are you doing? Haven't seen you **in a dog's age** — not since Arbor Day. Boy, we planted plenty of trees that day. We **worked ourselves to the bone**, didn't we? Now let me ask you about my Tommy. I

don't know what's up, but his teacher has contacted me with complaints...

Do you see how those clichés not only lower the level of the writing but also up the informality quotient?

Another way that informality can badly infect a piece of writing is when the writer indulges in qualifier abuse. Writers have very little reason to ever rely on qualifiers like *really*, *truly*, *kind of*, and *sort of*. When I see a high volume of such qualifiers in a piece, it is difficult for me to see anything else. A haze envelops the writing — a tentative, even apologetic haze that undercuts the work altogether. Your word processor's spelling and grammar checker will pick up on that issue, as it highlights certain words and phrases and counsels you to "consider more concise writing."

Of course, sometimes spelling and grammar checkers can be annoying, and you may want to retain your qualifier for whatever good and specific reason you may have (there are such occasions), but, that said, do pay attention to that "consider more concise writing" message to ensure that you are not using qualifiers as a crutch. Your writing should be able to stand on its own, without any reliance on *really*, *kind of*, or *sort of*.

Your writing is more likely to assume too informal a feeling because of word choice, but it often errs on the side of formality because of sentence structure. A shaky grasp on sentence structure can easily lead an insecure writer to lapse into awkward, stiff constructions that sound "right" to untutored ears. People who are taught to write by the rule book may never have had the chance to develop a good ear, so they are more inclined to go in a direction that sounds formal and, by extension, "proper." (but actually fusty. Remember that word?)

When writers lack confidence, they are also likely to fall into a passive rather than an active voice. It is an odd but prevalent phenomenon. Let me explain the difference between these two voices. When a sentence is written using the active voice, somebody or something is performing an action. When a sentence is written using the passive voice, the action is being done *to* somebody or something. Here are some examples, active first, then passive:

> Cookie jars lined Helen's kitchen.
>
> *Helen's kitchen was lined with cookie jars.*
>
> Jeremy attended Lisa's wedding.
>
> *Lisa's wedding was attended by Jeremy.*
>
> Hercule Poirot solved many mysteries.
>
> *Many mysteries were solved by Hercule Poirot.*

Try reading those sentences aloud, and I guarantee you will prefer the first version of each pair, the active voice. Any reader would. Readers like to hear about action, so a passive posture never feels as attractive.

If that's the case, then why do so many inexperienced writers fall into the passive voice? My theory is that the passive voice reflects their timidity. Being *done to* can feel more comfortable than *doing* — especially when the doing (as in writing) does not come naturally. But, as I say, readers don't like the passive voice. It makes them feel as though they are in the hands of a timid writer. Also, you should know that your spellchecker will point out passive constructions as well as the aforesaid instances of nonconcise writing. Use this tool freely to capture and correct that problem.

Let me give you another example of how a certain kind of construction emerges out of a lack of writing confidence and can convey a feeling of formality that could be off-putting to readers. I am thinking of constructions that use the phrase *to be*. Consider these examples:

> I found *La La Land* to be a very entertaining film.
>
> I would like there to be better rail service in New York State.
>
> In order to be a good driver, you need to drive defensively.

Each of those sentences has a distinctly clunky/stuffy feeling. Otherwise put, they feel as though they contain too many words to too little purpose.

Look at how those sentences can be rewritten to make them more fluid and dynamic:

> *La La Land* is a highly entertaining film.
>
> New York State needs better rail service.
>
> Good drivers know how to drive defensively.

Note how the passive and stuffy feeling that develops when you use the construction *to be* has fallen away. What is left is clean and muscular writing that makes each of these sentences easy to read and absorb.

Please understand that I am not coming down heavily against either informal or formal writing. As I said before, there is a time and a place for informal writing, and the same goes for formal writing. Problems occur when writers cannot control their tone, and in such cases the informal bleeds over into the formal or the formal clogs up the informal. Moving ahead, we will now consider how your choice of words and expressions can also affect tone.

## Metaphors and Similes

Metaphors and similes, which are figures of speech used to describe a thing by comparing it with something else, are unquestionably among the great writing tools. A metaphor simply calls one thing another, while a simile spells it out for you using *like* or *as*. Both are designed to enhance the level of meaning in a given text.

Metaphors and similes, used correctly, have incredible descriptive power. Instead of saying, "Julie had blue eyes that sparkled in the light and had a clarity that was remarkable," which is wordy without being vivid, you might say, "Julie's eyes were two blue crystals that caught the light." Okay, not a prizewinning metaphor, but perhaps better than the wordy version that came before. However, if you're unsure about the value of your metaphor, then don't use it, because stale metaphors are worse than no metaphors. With regard to "Julie's eyes," I would keep working at that metaphor until I found something better. I wouldn't invest a huge amount of time in it, but I'd give it two or three more tries.

In any event, that rather flat metaphor is nonetheless a true metaphor, as Julie's eyes are referred to as something other than what they actually are ("blue crystals"). If the sentence read, "Julie's eyes were *like* two blue crystals that caught the light," then you would have a simile, a metaphor in which a comparison is made using the word *like* or its equivalent.

Why would you choose to use metaphors and similes? Mostly, for economy (i.e., to avoid wordy descriptions) and to advance the power and originality of your writing. A powerful metaphor allows readers to visualize something in a new way and to make associations that enhance meaning. Great literature is full of great metaphors and similes. Consider these:

> A hot wind was blowing around my head, the strands of my hair lifting and swirling in it, like ink spilled in water.
>
> — *The Blind Assassin*, Margaret Atwood

> Her eyes look like lamps blaring up just before the oil is gone.
>
> — *As I Lay Dying*, William Faulkner

> A shutter, like the leathern eyelid of a lizard, flickered over the intensity of his gaze.
>
> — *To the Lighthouse*, Virginia Woolf

She tried to get rid of the kitten which had scrambled up her back and stuck like a burr just out of reach.
— *Little Women*, Louisa May Alcott

The elegant black-and-white ship, all 24,170 tons of it, loomed like a mountain in a dinner jacket.
— *The Amazing Adventures of Kavalier & Clay*, Michael Chabon

We read great literature with the expectation that we will discover such transcendent metaphors. We do not expect them in the writing of the layperson, however. As I have said all along the way, no reader is going to hold good, clean, simple language against you, so don't feel compelled to use metaphors and similes. But if you try, please note that they may go awry in significant ways. One of the most common transgressions is to use metaphors that are clichés.

## Clichés, Jargon, and Other Traps

Often, I'll be asked to edit writing that is absolutely crammed with clichés. In such pieces, everyone is an eager beaver with their ear to the ground and a chip on their shoulder. They are tilting at windmills, putting all their eggs in one basket, banging their heads against a brick wall, keeping their fingers crossed, and on and on and *on*. Nothing feels real or authentic in such writing. It all feels prepackaged and airless.

How can you recognize if something is a cliché? Easy enough. If it sounds overly familiar to your ear, it's because you've heard it over and over again — for years.

Busy as a bee
Labor of love
All thumbs
Leaps and bounds
Cute as a button
Mark my words
Moment of truth
Dime a dozen
No stone unturned
Fit as a fiddle
On pins and needles
Pure as the driven snow
Wake-up call
Tried and true

Such expressions are like wallpaper (that's a simile, by the way). They go in one eye and out the other (cliché, with a twist). As a rule of thumb (cliché), when it comes to metaphors, if they don't sound fresh as a daisy (cliché), don't use them. A cliché is an expression whose time has come and gone (cliché), but is still hanging around. Clichés will do nothing to enhance your writing. Instead, they signify a distinct paucity of imagination.

In essence, they are a crutch for writers who lack confidence. They represent a default position to which such writers can rush, leaving behind their insecurity if only for a moment while they remain falsely sheltered in the bosom of these tired and worn phrases. It is best to discard them (as you manage to hear them) and to replace them with fresher metaphors — or no metaphors at all.

Another kind of metaphorical construction that can

overwhelm your writing with almost viral rapacity is jargon. Jargon can be thought of as the language of the day (sometimes the language of the moment). It emanates from the various worlds that make up our culture — business, sports, entertainment, politics, law, technology — and it dates faster than cottage cheese.

Not only does jargon age quickly, but because it is the specialized language of a particular profession, trade, or group of people, it often takes on a tone that feels "in," leaving the reader "out." In other words, it can sound smug and excluding. In response, the hoi polloi pick up on it, as they attempt to jump on the cool-sounding bandwagon, and suddenly the butcher, the baker, and the candlestick maker (cliché) are talking about low-hanging fruit, wardrobe malfunctions, and thinking outside the box. Suddenly, the phrase "thinking outside the box" becomes antithetical to the concept behind the phrase, which is about innovation and originality, and instead signals the most tired kind of expression that, again, serves as nothing but wallpaper for the mind.

If you are going to try to control your tone, then you must attune your ear to jargon. And keep in mind that, with the internet and our twenty-four-hour news cycle, jargon has a greater capacity than ever to spread through the culture. Let me give you some additional examples of jargon from just a few of the various worlds that they spring from:

**Entertainment**

Greenlight
In the can

Cliff-hanger
Drama queen
Diva
Bad hair day

### Sports

Down for the count
Come out swinging
The gloves are off
Go the distance
Lead with one's chin
Throw in the towel
No holds barred
Hit it out of the park
Roll with the punches
Slam dunk
Sucker punch

### Business Jargon

Bang for the buck
Sweat equity
Due diligence
Chief cook and bottle washer
Get your ducks in a row
Face time
Buy-in
Move the needle

The occasional use of jargon and even the occasional cliché is not a fatal error. When working in a conversational

tone, aimed more at informality than formality, we are all inclined to throw in a "rule of thumb" or a "second to none" now and then, and such expressions will probably be absorbed by most of your audience without any real disapproval or even notice. You do want to stay away, however, from expressions that are more clearly hackneyed, which are legion, from "an ax to grind" to "you only live once" to "sigh of relief" to "plain as day." The trick, again, is to train yourself to hear those expressions that our ears have been taught to tolerate. That is not easy.

Let us also consider jargon that should never have been allowed to bridge the gulf between the profession that spawned it and the wider culture to which it has spread. I am thinking of legal language. Some find it hard to defend the use of legal language, even in legal situations. Law professor Richard Wydick wrote a bestselling book called *Plain English for Lawyers*, whose title is self-explanatory.

It is enough of a problem when lawyers use legal language where plain English would do, but it is even more of a problem when a layperson does. Usually, this is done to make one's writing sound "important" and "proper." Instead, the writing ends up stiff and dull. Here are some examples of the kind of "legalisms," noted in italics, that can clog up your writing and confuse your tone. The plain English versions follow in parentheses:

Phyllis *purchased* stockings at the five-and-dime. (Phyllis bought stockings at the five-and-dime.)

When you are ready, you may *commence* the test. (When you are ready, you may begin the test.)

It is important that you *comply* with the rules. (It is important that you follow the rules.)

Chris wasn't careful, and *consequently* he lost his way. (Chris wasn't careful, and so he lost his way.)

Paul put down a deposit on the apartment to *ensure* that he would get it. (Paul put down a deposit on the apartment to make sure he would get it.)

Jacqueline made *in excess of* $100,000 a year. (Jacqueline made more than $100,000 a year.)

Jack asked for *particulars* about the flight. (Jack asked for details about the flight.)

He lived in Toronto *prior to* living in Detroit. (He lived in Toronto before living in Detroit.)

Mrs. Walker talked to the dog walker *regarding* his schedule. (Mrs. Walker talked to the dog walker about his schedule.)

Elaine decided to *terminate* her relationship with Phil. (Elaine decided to end her relationship with Phil.)

Why, you ask, will this kind of legal language not work for you? Well, think back to the beginning of this step, when we discussed the issue of your *authentic voice* and how best to capture it. Now ask yourself: Is legal language reflective of your authentic voice? Who are you, after all? Atticus Finch? Perry Mason? No. You're you, so why are you trying to sound like a lawyer?

## Assorted Tonal Transgressions

Yes, there are even more ways to go wrong. We will only take a moment to point out one that you should be sure to sidestep. *You must never, ever use internet acronyms in your writing.* You know the ones I'm talking about — LOL, TBH, IMHO, FWIW, and such. Texting is not writing. Texting obviously has a place in the world, and I'm not knocking it, but you must never confuse it with writing. The only internet acronym you might be able to get away with in a real piece of writing is FAQ (Frequently Asked Questions). This has become so common, as in referring to a website or a brochure that has an FAQ section, that it has entered the language. One day, perhaps, LOL will do the same, but that is hopefully years off, if ever, and it is certainly not something you should be invoking now.

Another habit to avoid as best you can is relying on the gassy buzzwords that come from the nonprofit world, which have badly infected the common vernacular. Think about the fundraising letters that come from your alma mater, your local hospital, or other charities you have supported. Think about the language. Can you hear all those references to *empowerment, potential, goals, transformation, opportunity, commitment, competence,* and *passion?* As with legal language, people wrongheadedly try to lend some "importance" to their writing by using such bulky, self-important words. As a result, everybody today is "passionate" and "in quest of their goals" that they are pursuing with "commitment" as they look to "fulfill their potential." Yikes!

Although you can avoid these kinds of problems by relying on good, clean, simple, muscular writing (the kind, I keep telling you, that readers will never hold against you), I don't want you to think that I am against a more ambitious approach to writing. That would be absurd. Naturally, we all aspire to become better at the things we take on, whether it's golf, downhill skiing, or writing, and one manifestation of becoming a better writer is to handle more complex writing forms. After all, your writing represents a kind of continuum, and hopefully, over time, you will feel more comfortable creating complex sentences and be more observant of the tone you are trying to project. While you are working your way along this continuum, however, you can enrich your writing and build complexity with vocabulary.

## In Praise of Words

In Step Four, we talked about how much writers love sentences. Most writers I know have that same kind of love for words. In fact, it's hard to imagine a writer who doesn't love words. You don't have to be a professional writer, however, to love words. Words are free, they're completely available, there is no limitation on them, and they have the capacity to continually surprise and delight us. In fact, I think an early love for words exists in most people. That's one reason Dr. Seuss has remained so popular all these years. His talent for inventing vocabulary — *oobleck, grinch, zillow, kwigger, nizzard, diffendoofer* — is certainly one reason his work continues to find new generations of fans.

That early love for vocabulary and word acquisition is often squelched (good word) by outside influences, well-meaning or otherwise. A teacher who teaches vocabulary in ways that are uninspired and humdrum (nice word), demanding memorization of lists of words that stultify (fine word), can do a lifetime's amount of harm. Studying lists of words for standardized exams, like the SAT or the ACT, is also a dreaded experience for many people. I did that decades ago and have never used many of the words I was made to learn, like *uxorious*, *penurious*, and *termagant*.

You might well ask why a strong vocabulary is important to writing anyway. To that question, I would say that it allows you to find *the right word for what you are trying to express*. The French author Gustave Flaubert, whose *Madame Bovary* is one of the greatest novels ever written, was committed to finding *le mot juste* ("the right word"). He engaged in a process of continual pruning and would often spend a week or more turning out one meticulous page.

Such a level of commitment is exceedingly rare, and I am certainly not implying that you make that kind of commitment, but it is also worth recognizing that there is delight, even joy, in finding *le mot juste*. To be able to say that the reverend concluded with a "benediction" instead of "some final blessings" is to access the power of writing, which, as we said at the beginning of this book, is all about communication. To be able to say that the desk chair had "ergonomic" value is better than saying that the desk chair "was designed to promote efficiency and comfort in the workplace." Fewer words and more focus.

A particularly good example of how an enhanced vocabulary can improve your writing can be found in connection with the use of verbs. Flabby writing is often connected to an overreliance on adverbs, along the lines of these dim constructions:

> The mugger stood suspiciously in the shadows.
>
> Elizabeth's pupils widened noticeably from the eye drops.
>
> The puppy staunchly resisted its newspaper training.

A powerful vocabulary will allow you to replace those bulky adverbial constructions — "stood suspiciously," "widened noticeably," "staunchly resisted" — with strong verbs. Consider these alternatives:

> The mugger lurked in the shadows.
>
> The eye drops dilated Elizabeth's pupils. (Note too the change to the active voice.)
>
> The puppy balked at its newspaper training.

Fewer words, more focus, more interest. Let the verbs do their work — and collect powerful verbs like *lurk*, *dilate*, and *balk* to beef up your writing.

Keep in mind, however, that certain pitfalls can accompany your efforts to improve your vocabulary. An overreliance on the thesaurus will often lead people to use words that are inappropriate for the situation. In an effort to create writing that sounds "important," people sometimes wind up using words that make them sound stuffy, overly formal, or just plain confused. They throw around words like *grandiloquent* and *magnanimous*, captivated by their many syllables but unattuned to their nuances.

The nuances and connotations of words must always be kept in mind. If you go to a thesaurus and look up *old*, for instance, you'll get a word like *elderly*, which is a perfectly fine stand-in if you are referring to an older person, but you'll also get *archaic*. That is a word that is reserved for institutions or cultural behaviors or traditions, but not people. You would never call a person "archaic."

Despite such pitfalls, it is a good and worthwhile thing to work at developing your vocabulary, and that work goes even better if you can integrate it into your life rather than approaching it as a hardship to avoid. You can do that in a variety of ways. Chief among them is *word collection*.

Think of yourself as a collector. Just as you would collect seashells or stamps or coins, so can you collect words. Get into a serious reading habit with one or two sources that give you pleasure, whether it's the *Wall Street Journal* or *Rolling Stone* or *Scientific American*. Read an article or two a day. (Yes, you have time for that. Don't tell me otherwise.) Circle a few words that are new to you. Look them up in whatever dictionary, online or hard copy, you like to use. Write those one or two daily words down in your log, which you can keep on your phone, in a notebook, or wherever it best suits you. You will see your vocabulary start to build quickly that way.

You should also get into the habit of using a dictionary. Too often, we fall into the lazy habit of not looking up words we don't know. I confess: I do it too. To this day, I'm not sure what the word *louche* means, although I have seen it mentioned time and again in the articles I read. (Okay, I just guilted myself out and looked it up. *Louche* means "disreputable or sordid in a rakish and appealing way.") Clearly, *louche* is not one of your everyday words, but if I were looking for *le mot juste* to capture the quality of the rather seedy older gentleman in my community-theater production of *Arsenic and Old Lace*, *louche* could well be the word I was looking for.

When we read demanding material, the onslaught of difficult words might be more than we can handle, and that can bring on resistance that translates into torpor (nice word). Maintain your motivation as best you can to learn new words as they come up. In today's world, with all our devices, it isn't exactly hard to google them. Back in the day, when you had to find a Merriam-Webster, that was a different story, but now all of these words are right there at our fingertips.

If you enjoy games, as most people do, know too that you can learn many words by going that route. Playing Scrabble with someone who has a good vocabulary can be a revelation, and on your own you can take on increasingly more difficult crossword puzzles, which will surely be filled with words that are new to you.

Best of all is to read. And read. And read. In every respect, we learn invaluable lessons about writing from reading. Certainly, in the case of word acquisition, there is nothing like it. And with a vigorous program of word acquisition, you will have another tool by which you can control the tone of your writing.

## Don't Forget Dialogue

Before we step off this step, I want to alert you to one other means by which you can alter the tone of your writing, and that is dialogue. Most lay writers I know rarely think about using dialogue, which is not really all that surprising. To write good dialogue, you need to have a good ear. If you don't have a good ear for dialogue, the result will be tinny and awkward. But if you have a reasonable ear, which you can try to develop, then you can use dialogue to enliven your writing and "humanize" your tone.

When I work with students on their college-admission essays, I almost never see so much as a scrap of dialogue in their first draft. For example, I had a student who was writing about his experience on a rugby team and how it helped him fit in at a British boarding school, where he had enrolled as a foreign student. Here is a piece of action from that essay:

> After a short break, we were back at it, sprinting now in a diagonal line and passing the ball from one end to the other. Such drills taught us to work together and trust each other, allowing us to become a powerful entity rather than a conglomeration of strong-willed competitors.

Nothing wrong with that writing, but I suggested that he include a bit of dialogue to "warm it up." Since the story was about his integration into a community, some simple dialogue would seem to be a most appropriate way to capture the flavor of that community. He took my advice, and in the next draft that section looked like this:

> After a short break, we were back at it, this time sprinting in a diagonal line as we passed the ball. Such drills taught us to become a single powerful entity rather than

a conglomeration of strong-willed competitors. "Here,
Walter!" I shouted to my teammate. "Ship it right!"

He wound up using that kind of dialogue here and there
throughout the essay, always keeping it very simple, and it
certainly helped to get his essay across.

You don't have to be a Pulitzer Prize–winning playwright
to write dialogue. As I say, if you have a totally tin ear when
it comes to dialogue, it's probably better not to go down that
path (cliché), but if you decide you want to try your hand at
dialogue, do so with these two fundamental pointers in mind:

1. **Do not use dialogue for expository purposes.** Never
   have someone say something like, "Tomorrow I have
   to go to the bank to talk to the officer there about
   getting a loan for my cupcake business." That kind of
   dialogue will put your reader to sleep. Instead, use dialogue as a condiment for your writing — short and
   spicy, conveying emotions, not background details.
2. **Keep your attribution simple.** "'Here, Walter!' I shouted
   to my teammate" is infinitely better than "'Here,
   Walter!' I shouted furiously to my teammate" or
   "'Here, Walter!' I shouted desperately to my teammate." Attributions should be as "invisible" as possible. In fact, the word *said* will usually suffice, and
   you can leave the *murmured* and *gasped* and *sighed* at
   home. Most important, never add adverbs like *furiously* or *desperately* to the verbs in your attributions.
   That is poor writing form and should be avoided altogether.

If you're interested in dialogue and would like to try your hand at it, then it's a good idea to read the dialogue of a master. Try a play by David Mamet (*Glengarry Glen Ross*) or Aaron Sorkin (*A Few Good Men*), or curl up with a novel by Elmore Leonard (*Get Shorty*). And most important, listen consciously to the everyday talk of the people around you. Be an eavesdropper in the coffee shop, on the bus, in the bleachers, wherever you happen to be. Listen for patterns and rhythms. Human speech does not come out in long, perfectly formed, uninterrupted sentences (unless you're Hillary Clinton). It's a gloriously messy business, and therein lies the work involved in capturing it.

## Up Close

For this step, we're going to go really "up close" by looking at just a portion of text. It comes from a college-admission essay, and it shows just how wrong a writer can go with tone. This writer was a highly intelligent young man who submitted the following to me as the opening of the first draft of his essay:

> The air crackles with apprehension. The auditorium is utterly silent, save for the occasional sound of shuffling feet. I glance at my audience for a moment, breathing in the atmosphere and quelling my emotions and anxieties. I place my hands daintily on the glittering ivory keys. Then I begin. The powerful, four-note melody of Beethoven's 5th Symphony resounds brilliantly from the grand piano, supplanting the apprehensive mood

with excitement. As I play, my consciousness becomes bound to the majestic crescendos and vibrant melodies that expunge themselves into the air, evoking memories of courage and of the risks that I have embraced.

The soft smell of musty wood slithers into my nostrils. I am in the basement of my instructor's home. I place my hands on the opaque keys of his ancient piano and begin. The harsh dissonance of incorrect notes pierce the silence. I can barely make it past the first bar. "Perhaps you are not ready for this. We should try a different song. An easier one." The words sting. They lacerate my very confidence, bruising me in a way no insult or physical malady ever could.

I have heard this sentence my whole life. My mind flashes back to the eighth grade. "You will never be good at math. You will do poorly in high school, Raymond," says my math instructor, a sneer of distaste on her face. A slight smile touches my lips as I remember further. I see my ninth-grade transcript: I have straight As in math. The memory ignites a passion within me, an insatiable desire to prove my instructor wrong. I shall forge my own path. I am afraid but determined. I turn to my instructor, my consciousness cleared and set to purpose. "I can do this," I say. "Just let me try."

As I play upon the gazes of a mesmerized audience, the powerful majestic melody sings to me a tune of my courage, of a willingness to embrace what a superior thought impossible. Its domineering and commanding tune parallels how I suppressed any doubts or discouraging remarks and instead trusted in my own instinct to lead me to the success I achieved.

Whoa. I'm sure you felt, as I did, that this was a heavy slough. Looking at the tone of this text, what would you say are the characteristics that distinguish the voice of this writer? Some that I thought of are: melodramatic, self-pitying, pretentious, and overwrought. Obviously, none of those characteristics are attractive, and the pity of it is that once this young man got over his case of nerves and settled into his authentic voice, he was a perfectly likable fellow. But that's what writing can do to some people. It can make them nervous, cause them to sound inauthentic, and make them come off like someone you'd rather not know.

One other word that I would apply to this text is *florid*. The original meaning of florid is "covered with flowers." That meaning is now considered obsolete, and these days *florid* is mostly used to describe someone who is ruddy ("the stout man had a florid complexion") or a writing style that is marked by overly complicated rhetorical devices or self-consciously unusual words ("With his love for polysyllabic words, Mr. Evans was known for his florid writing").

The problems in that lengthy paragraph cited above start right at the beginning:

The air crackles with apprehension.

That's a good example of what can happen when a writer focuses more on tone than on communication. For starters, *air*, used here as a subject, cannot be apprehensive. Air does not have any cognitive faculties, so it cannot experience emotions like hate, love, or fear (apprehension).

The use of the word *crackles* compounds the problems

in that sentence. That word leaves readers scratching their heads. Does something that is apprehensive (putting aside for the moment that air *can't* be apprehensive) crackle? A fire crackles. The lungs can crackle. I'm not sure that air crackles or, if it does, whether apprehension would be the agent involved.

Let's continue:

> The air crackles with apprehension. The auditorium is utterly silent, save for the occasional sound of shuffling feet. I glance at my audience for a moment, breathing in the atmosphere and quelling my emotions and anxieties. I place my hands daintily on the glittering ivory keys. Then I begin.

I see no problems with that second sentence, but in the third sentence the overwrought, melodramatic, and florid qualities return. Can you, in fact, "breathe in the atmosphere," as cited in the third sentence? Sounds awkward to my ears. "Quelling my emotions and anxieties"? Not exactly wrong — but vaguely pretentious.

Then, in the next sentence, the writer places his hands "daintily" on the glittering ivory keys — and this leads me to suspect that he has no real understanding of the nuances of the word *dainty*, because if he did, I don't think he would have used it. *Dainty* means either "delicately small and pretty" (like a lace handkerchief or a porcelain figurine) or "fastidious and difficult to please" ("Portia had a dainty appetite and would never think of eating with her fingers"). Did he mean *tentatively*? I could imagine him "tentatively" placing his hands on the glittering ivory keys. (Oh, and by the way, ivory doesn't glitter. Gold glitters. Ivory has a soft sheen.)

Moving right along, let's examine this section:

> As I play, my consciousness becomes bound to the majestic crescendos and vibrant melodies that expunge themselves into the air, evoking memories of courage and of the risks that I have embraced.

At this point the tone of this piece begins to develop some very serious problems. The very likable young man who wrote this starts to feel less likable when he tries to impress the reader with fancy words and outsized emotions. Also, when I read about "majestic crescendos and vibrant melodies that expunge themselves," I question the word choice. After all, *expunge* means to "erase or completely remove something unwanted or unpleasant," as in expunging an offense from one's record, so that is clearly an incorrect word choice.

All told, this is a writer who is trying way too hard. And by overexerting himself to this extent, his writing becomes increasingly chaotic as he goes along:

> The soft smell of musty wood slithers into my nostrils.

Does he mean the wood from the piano? That wouldn't be *musty*, meaning "having a stale, moldy, or damp smell," unless the piano has been sitting outside in a monsoon. And since when does a smell "slither" into one's nostrils? (Snakes slither. Smells? Not so much.)

The next section becomes more narrative in feeling. His instructor suggests that the piece might be too difficult for him and that perhaps he should try something easier. This brings back a stinging memory of a math teacher in eighth grade who also questioned his abilities and whom he disproved by getting straight As in math in ninth grade. We're not liking this writer any better, because the content has become both self-pitying and vengeful at the same time, but the narrative pull at least seems to be helping to control the writing a bit more. As the writer goes back into the present action of the piece, confronting the doubting music instructor, things fall apart again and the full extent of the self-importance and aggrandizement takes over with these words:

> As I play upon the gazes of a mesmerized audience, the powerful majestic melody sings to me a tune of my courage, of a willingness to embrace what a superior thought impossible. Its domineering and commanding tune parallels how I suppressed any doubts or discouraging remarks and instead trusted in my own instinct to lead me to the success I achieved.

Now, think about what he is actually saying here. As he plays "upon the gazes of a mesmerized audience," which is overblown, the "powerful majestic melody" becomes a "tune of my courage." Oh, really? Could this possibly sound more self-important?

The point of this is not to show how snarky one can be about another person's writing. I always work under the assumption that every one of my student writers can achieve a level of excellence, and if they work at the process, they do. The point of this is to show the disastrous effect that tonal inconsistencies and tonal transgressions can have on a piece of writing.

I made a judgment call with this writer. I said to him, point blank, that his writing on this assignment was poor. I decided to go with shock therapy. To his credit, he took it like a champ. We threw out this essay entirely, and we found another, likable subject to write about. (He wrote about the preconceptions that his friends had of his having to perform at the highest levels academically solely because he was Asian, and he was smart and funny and perceptive about it.)

He and I became committed collaborators and wound up liking each other very much. He went to Dartmouth and has had a very successful time of it. And why not? He was, as I've said, a smart and likable young man. I simply couldn't allow his writing to undo that — and I have reason to believe that, going forward, he will avoid writing whose tone makes him sound like someone he isn't.

## ROUNDUP

1. One of your primary goals as a writer is to capture your authentic voice. Tone becomes a significant issue in writing when it takes you away from that.

2. You are encouraged to try a diagnostic exercise to identify the characteristics of your authentic voice — and to adjust those characteristics if need be.

3. Writers often grapple with a tone that is overly formal or informal.

4. Informality rears its head with imperatives, contractions, qualifiers, and the use of colloquial words and expressions.

5. One way that formality intrudes is when writers lapse into the passive voice.

6. Metaphors and similes are useful writing tools, but can also lead writers into clichés and jargon, which can badly affect tone.

7. In order to eliminate clichés and jargon, writers must train themselves to "hear" stale expressions that the ear has been taught to tolerate.

8. Never use internet acronyms in your writing.

9. A solid vocabulary is a helpful tool in controlling tone.

10. Word collection, regularly using a dictionary, playing word games, and, most of all, reading are excellent ways to develop your vocabulary.

11. Dialogue is another way to alter and control the tone of a piece of writing. The two cardinal rules for the writing of dialogue are to never use dialogue for expository purposes and to always keep attributions simple.

# STEP SEVEN

# Do the Lapidary Work

S ome pages back, we discussed the value of a strong vocabulary. Now we come to a case in point: *lapidary*. *Lapidary*,
as defined by *Webster's Universal College Dictionary*, means
"characterized by an exactitude and extreme refinement that
suggests gem cutting." Nice word. And most fitting for the
writing goals we are setting for ourselves.

In this last step, we are concentrating on the very de-
tailed, close-up work that will make the difference between a
piece that is okay and a piece that is outstanding. In working
with college applicants, I am struck by how fascinated and
surprised they are by the amount of attention that goes into
a piece of writing. When they get drafts back from me, at
least for the first two or three go-rounds, those drafts are covered with red, and I tell them not to be shocked or shamed
by what they are seeing, because this is what happens when
an editor gets involved in the writing process. In fact, when I

send something to an editor, my work often comes back with just as many notes and corrections as they are seeing on their work.

Unquestionably, hiring an editor to work on a piece of writing is a luxury. One might indulge in such a luxury to try to gain acceptance at a top school or to bring a piece of writing to a point at which a publisher might want to publish it. Editorial services are expensive, however, and not always reliable, so your goal here is to become your own editor. You may not become brilliant at the job, but with careful focus you can certainly become much better at it.

When I edit a piece of writing, I look at the broad-stroke issues first. Does the structure make sense? Is the point of view the best choice for the piece? (That is, would the piece work better in first or third person? In past or present tense?) Is the tone consistent or does it wobble around? These are exactly the issues we've been talking about in all the previous steps of this book.

Here, as the work moves toward its final draft, we focus on the lapidary work. We look at word choice, punctuation, and spelling, and we try to make everything as good as it can be. In this step, we are casting our most critical eye on the piece to catch as many mistakes and weak spots as we can.

## Persistent Pruning

All along, we've been talking about the implicit contract between writer and reader, which dictates that the former will not squander the time of the latter. As you get into the end run, don't lose sight of that contract. There is always more that you can take out, and pruning away any unnecessary words will build goodwill with your readers. Otherwise put, the fewer words, the better. (Apologies to James Joyce and Thomas Pynchon.) Seriously, however, most readers regard spare writing as good writing. If I've said this before, bear with me because I want to say it again: *A reader will never hold clean, simple writing against you.*

College-admission essays almost always have word limits. Some essays have a limit of 100 words; others, 250; still others, 650. My students and I never go over the word limit for the simple reason that *we don't know what will happen if we do.* In fact, perhaps nothing will happen if you're 10 words over the limit, but why risk it? Whenever students send me late-stage drafts that are 50 to 75 words over the limit, I reduce their word count through "invisible cuts." These are words and phrases I can remove because they are so insignificant and unnecessary that my student writers can't even detect them. You can do the same with your writing if you put your mind to it.

Let's remind ourselves of some areas and issues that call out for pruning:

- **Minimize adjectives and adverbs.** I have amply expressed my lack of enthusiasm for adjectives and adverbs, which, as far as I'm concerned, clog things up. Remember our rule about replacing a weak adverbial phrase like *stood suspiciously* with a strong action verb like *lurked?* Keep that advice in mind, and you'll save words all over the place. Similarly, ask yourself if you need that adjective describing the man in the toll booth (*swarthy*, *rotund*, or whatever else you've stolen out of a thesaurus). A good rule of thumb is to question *every* adjective and adverb, asking yourself if you need it or if things would be just fine without it.

Qualifiers like *very* or *just* or *really* are also easy cuts to make. We referred to them earlier and identified them as words that signal insecure writing. You don't need them — nor does your reader. As with those weak adverbial phrases that can be replaced by strong verbs, sentences with qualifiers can be rewritten and made stronger with better word choices. For instance, a sentence like "It is very hard to make a soufflé" can be changed to "It is difficult to make a soufflé." "It is really simple to fry an egg" can become "It is easy to fry an egg." Remember too that some words are not eligible for qualifiers at all. One mistake that particularly irks English teachers is to refer to something as "very unique." Something is either unique or it isn't; there's no such thing as "very unique."

- **Avoid pairs.** I often work with writers who want to use two of everything. Their writing is sprinkled with phrases like "each and every," "without regret or remorse," "he expressed sympathy and compassion," and "the day was fair and pleasant." As with qualifiers, such constructions bespeak the insecure writer. They cry out "insurance": because the writer feels less than confident about describing the day as "fair," he adds "pleasant" for insurance. That kind of decision making belongs to earlier drafts. By the time you get to advanced drafts, you should be using language that doesn't require the constant sprinkling of synonyms.

- **Don't say the same thing twice.** I can't tell you how often I edit out repetition. People will do a fine job of making a point — and then they'll make it again. Writers prone to this often do the same with several points. Call it insecurity, but whatever label it goes by, it's a chore for readers.

- **Don't dither.** To *dither* means "to be indecisive, falter, waver, hesitate, or vacillate." I see my student writers dithering all the time. They often start sentences with, "It seems," "I think," "It is safe to say," or any of those wishy-washy expressions that convey tentativeness. Instead, just jump in.

- **Steer clear of the passive voice.** "The flat tire was changed by Jim." "The casserole was prepared by Brenda." "The house was destroyed by termites." We previously discussed how the passive voice affects tone, but the passive voice also tends to use more words — and uses up more of the reader's time. If you rewrite the sentences above in the active voice — "Jim changed the flat tire," "Brenda prepared a casserole," "Termites destroyed the house" — then you'll see that those three active sentences taken together add up to 13 words, compared to the 19 words those three sentences take up in the passive voice. The active voice offers a savings of 6 words. Does a savings of 6 words even matter to the reader? You'd be surprised.

- **Avoid nominalizations.** Never heard of a nominalization? It's a verb that is reshaped to take on the qualities of a noun. For instance, you might write, "Howard Carter made the discovery of King Tut's tomb in 1922" (11 words), instead of the simpler, "Howard Carter discovered King Tut's tomb in 1922" (8 words). Or perhaps, "Robert Mueller conducted an investigation of Russian collusion in the 2016 election" (12 words) instead of "Robert Mueller investigated Russian collusion in the 2016 election" (9 words). Endings like *-ment, -ant, -ency, -ance, -ity,* and *-tion* are indicators that nominalizations are lurking in your writing, giving it a doughy quality that is exactly the opposite of what you should be striving for.
- **Stay positive.** Negative constructions not only sound, well, negative, but they also use more words. "There were not many people in the audience" uses more words than "There were few people in the audience" or "It was an audience of very few." Consider this sentence: "The instruction booklet for the refrigerator did not include tips on defrosting" (12 words). Now consider this rewrite: "The instruction booklet for the refrigerator omitted tips on defrosting" (10 words). Two fewer words might seem inconsequential, but everything adds up in a piece of writing — and it's also nice to weed out that negative tone.

Making your writing more concise is an important focus of the lapidary work in which you are involved at this point in the writing process. The more you learn to train a practiced eye on your writing, the more you can shape your prose so that nothing on the page is wasted.

## Vague Pronouns

Another focus of your lapidary work is to rid your writing of vague pronouns. Although we have covered pronouns before, let's refresh our memory. A pronoun is that part of speech that exists to replace a noun. Pronouns are eminently useful, keeping us from having to read sentences like, "The Goodmans introduced the Goodmans to their neighbors." Instead, pronouns allow us to rewrite that sentence as, "The Goodmans introduced themselves to their neighbors." *Themselves* is the pronoun that allows us to avoid repeating the words *the Goodmans*. So, as Martha Stewart might say, pronouns are "a good thing," but that doesn't mean they are trouble-free. A particular problem occurs with *vague pronouns*.

Vague pronouns litter the work of some of my student writers who think they can put *it*, *their*, or *this* wherever they want, and I'm going to know what they're talking about. Not so. If a reader is left wondering to what or whom a pronoun refers, then you can be sure that the problem is a vague pronoun.

Let's look at an example of a sentence that contains a vague pronoun and see how to fix it:

The coaches told the players that they had work to do if they wanted to get ready for the Sunday game.

Do you have any idea who *they* refers to in this sentence? Is it the coaches or the players who have a lot of work to do? *They* in this sentence is distinctly vague, and it needs to be rewritten to solve that problem. (Aha! There you have a prime example of a vague pronoun. What is *it* referring to in the sentence you just read? You don't know, right? So I will rewrite that sentence: "*They* in this sentence is distinctly vague, and the sentence needs to be rewritten to solve that problem." Can you see that I fixed the sentence simply by repeating the word *sentence?*)

Now, getting back to the sentence about the coaches and the players, here is a possible fix:

> The coaches told the players that hard work was needed
> to get ready for the Sunday game.

In that version, all the pronouns are eliminated and the idea of working hard embraces both coaches and players. Nice, and democratic.

Here's another fix:

> The coaches told the players to work hard to get ready
> for the Sunday game.

Again, we see that the pronouns have been eliminated but the meaning has been altered. In this "less democratic" version, the "hard work" is assigned exclusively to the players.

One way to identify vague pronouns is to look through your writing, circle words like *it*, *which*, *they*, *this*, and *that*, and connect them back to their antecedents. (The antecedent is the word the pronoun replaces. For example, in the sentence, "The dog loved its bed," the antecedent is *the dog*, which is replaced by the pronoun *its*. Without that pronoun, the sentence would have to read: "The dog loved the dog's bed." Not good.) If you find the antecedent missing, then you must go back and rewrite the sentence, making sure that there is a clear antecedent, so that the pronoun you have used to replace it will not be seen as vague.

A virtually surefire way to fall into the vague-pronoun trap is to start a sentence with the word *It*. As a rule, you would do better to repeat a word, running the risk of some redundancy, than to start a sentence that way.

## Exorcising Demons

Every book I have written about writing — and this is the third — has contained a section on the most common technical errors that writers make. Eradicating these mistakes is not rocket science (cliché). In fact, all that is required is some concentration and the will to make your writing better. To that end, let's move on to this section in which I name my Top Twenty most avoidable mistakes and tell you how to spot and solve them. Here we go.

### 1. *their, there*

Word-processing tools like spellchecker and grammar checker can certainly help you spot errors. It is important to remember, however, that these tools are far from foolproof. They won't pick up incorrect usage of words that are spelled correctly, for instance. So if you have a *their* where a *there* should be, spellchecker is likely to miss that altogether. Therefore, it is essential that you understand the difference between these two words.

*There* is a noun signifying "that place, position, or point" or an adverb meaning "in, at, or to that place":

I went there with a heavy heart.

There but for the grace of God go I.

Venice is packed in the summer, but if you go there in the winter it is beautiful in a desolate way.

*Their*, on the other hand, is an entirely different word with an entirely different meaning. *Their* is a possessive adjective. Possessive adjectives — which include *my*, *his*, *her*, *its*, *our*, and *your* — signify possession of something. Here are examples of sentences in which the word *their* is used correctly as a possessive adjective:

They arranged their chairs in a circle.

Working mothers have a lot on their plates.

Laurel and Hardy were famous for their meticulously worked-out routines.

What about *theirs*? *Theirs* is a possessive pronoun (others are *mine*, *his*, *hers*, *its*, *ours*, and *yours*). *Theirs*, used in a sentence, looks like this (and note that this sentence uses both the possessive pronoun *theirs* and the possessive adjective *their*):

Jack and Maria toured Jerusalem all day with their travel group, but the evening was theirs to do with as they wished.

Learning the difference between *there* and *their* is simple enough, so don't allow the misuse of those words to drag down the level of your writing.

## 2. *it's, its*

As long as we're talking about possessive pronouns, let's look at one — *its* — and differentiate it from *it's*. *It's* is a contraction that, like most contractions, is formed by eliminating certain letters and replacing them with an apostrophe. *You don't* is a contraction of *You do not*. *She can't* is a contraction of *She cannot*. *It's* is a contraction of *It is*.

Also, while we're on the subject, some people seem to think that using contractions in writing is a problem. In everything but the most formal writing — let's say an academic thesis — it's entirely okay to use contractions. Perhaps you'll want to restrict the flow of them in certain pieces of writing, but as you have seen in this book, I have used them regularly, but not always. In other words, a constant flow of contractions can be distracting, so writers must rely on their ear to gauge the right number of contractions.

But getting back to the issue at stake here, *it's* is a contraction standing for *it is*, while *its* is a possessive pronoun. Here are some examples of the correct use of *it's* and *its*:

It's laundry day in the Stevenson household. ("It is laundry day" is the uncontracted form of that phrase.)

Children love the story of how the leopard got its spots. (*Its* is the possessive pronoun, as the spots belong to, or are possessed by, the leopard.)

It's funny to see Westerners trying to use chopsticks. ("It is funny" is the uncontracted form of that phrase.)

The winter storm held the city in its grip. (*Its* is the possessive pronoun signifying that the grip that the city is in belongs to the winter storm.)

So, like *their/there*, we have an example of two words that mean totally different things, but that are often used interchangeably and wrongly. Indeed, I cannot tell you how often I see sentences like "The winter storm held the city in it's grip" instead of its correct version above. This is a technical issue that can be cleared up quite simply with just a little focused concentration, and it would save writer, reader, and editor so much extra effort.

### 3. then, than

Here is another example of the kind of confusion that was set off for people in third or fourth grade — one that they never bothered to address and that can continue to dog their writing for the rest of their lives. *Then* and *than* are two words, like *their/there* and *it's/its*, that have entirely different meanings, but that are often used interchangeably. Indeed, I have worked with writers who have used both *then* and *than* incorrectly in the same paragraph.

*Then* is a conjunctive adverb. A conjunction is a part of speech that connects phrases and clauses (like *and* or *but*). When that job of connecting ideas falls to an adverb, that word becomes a conjunctive adverb. Examples of conjunctive adverbs include *otherwise, finally, meanwhile, moreover, next, therefore, thus, indeed,* and *however.* (There are many more.) Here is an example of how the conjunctive adverb *then* is used in a sentence:

> I went to the opera; then, to my delight, I was invited to the ballet the following night.

Another way to understand *then* and use it correctly is to appreciate the different meanings it carries. *Then* can mean

> "at a certain time," as in, "If you can wait until later, I'll be ready then."
>
> a moment in a time sequence, as in, "We went to a movie and then had dinner."
>
> "in addition to," as in, "The traffic and the noise in the city is bad enough, and then there is the smog."
>
> "as a result of" or "accordingly," as in, "If I don't get to the restaurant in time, then they won't hold my table."

It is safe to say that virtually every time you see the word *then*, it will be used as a conjunctive adverb, suggesting one of those four meanings.

On much rarer occasions, *then* can also be used as an adjective, as in, "Social Security was instituted in 1935 by then president Franklin D. Roosevelt."

The word *than*, as we have indicated, has an entirely different meaning (and an entirely different vowel). *Than* is a conjunction, which we discussed above (i.e., a word that connects clauses or phrases), and is used primarily to make comparisons: "My dog is bigger than your dog," "Kevin runs faster than Russell," or "Most historians regard Lincoln as a greater president than Washington."

One good way to check your writing to make sure that you have used *then* and *than* correctly is to understand that there is no synonym for *than*. *Then* has many synonyms (e.g., *subsequently*, *also*; see the meanings given above). I defy you, however, to come up with a synonym for *than* in the sentence "My dog is bigger than your dog." You might come up with a dense cluster of words — "My dog is bigger in relative proportion to your dog," let's say — but that is inconsistent with the idea of a conjunction, which is designed to create fewer words, not more. So if you see the word *than* and can't think of a substitute, you can tell yourself that you have used it correctly.

### 4. lose, loose

Here's an easy one — but you'd be surprised how many people get it wrong. The trick to getting *lose/loose* right is to *listen* to the sounds that these two words make. The word *lose*, which means to "be deprived of or cease to have" ("Jim will lose his job if he doesn't improve") or "become unable to find" ("If he doesn't pay attention, Jim will lose his keys"), rhymes with *ooze*, *booze*, *choose*, and *news*.

The word *loose*, which means "not firmly or tightly fixed in place" ("Jim went to the dentist to get a loose tooth taken care of"), has a hissy sound that rhymes with *goose*, *noose*, and *juice*. When you see either of these words on the page, sound them out to make sure that you've selected the right one for your purpose.

### 5. affect, effect

I will wager that if you ask ten people on the street to use either *affect* or *effect* in a sentence, eight of them will get it wrong. In truth, this one is rather complicated, so let's roll up our sleeves and sort it out.

*Affect* and *effect* are two words that have four distinct meanings. Let me run through them:

- *Affect.* When the accent is on the final syllable (a-FECT), you have a verb that means "to have an influence on."

  Obesity can affect (a-FECT) your heart.

  Unemployment will affect (a-FECT) voter turnout this year.

- *Affect.* When the accent is on the first syllable (AFF-ect), *affect* is a noun that means "emotion." This use is rare, and unless you read psychological case histories featuring sentences like "James W. had little visible affect" (AFF-ect), you may never encounter this use of the word.
- *Effect.* Most commonly, *effect* is a noun that means "a change that is a result or consequence of an action or other cause," as in:

Liquor had a bad effect on his driving.

One effect of overpopulation on sub-Saharan Africa is a shortage of food.

*Effect* as a noun can also mean "the lighting, sound, or scenery used in a play, movie, or broadcast." Here it is, shown in the plural: "The special effects of the latest Star Wars movie were dazzling."

- *Effect*. As with *affect*, *effect* also comes in a rarer form in which it is used as a verb meaning "to cause something to happen or to bring something about." Here are a couple of examples of that usage:

The new policy study will surely effect change in the penal system.

Harriet Tubman was committed to effecting social reform.

Unlike *affect*, all versions of *effect* sound the same when spoken. One way you can begin to get a handle on this complicated picture is by looking at your use of the words *affect* and *effect* on the page. If you are using *affect* as a noun and *effect* as a verb, then it is likely that you are getting those words wrong.

### 6. a lot, allot, alot

Here's another easy one. There is no such word as *alot*. You won't find it in any dictionary. The correct form, *a lot*, means "much of something."

Joshua had a lot of candy in his bag.

My uncle knows a lot about world geography.

It takes a lot to make me jealous.

If that nonword *alot* had one additional letter, however, we would have the word *allot*, which means "to divide or distribute by share or portion." The word *allot* is used correctly in these sentences:

Each farmer was allotted his share of seed.

My church allots a portion of its mission fund to the local food pantry.

The law should not allot blame equally if the responsibilities of the individuals involved vary.

Again, as with *lose / loose*, just a few minutes of focused concentration should clear things up and prevent you from repeatedly making the same mistake.

## 7. *good, well*

Another mind bender that afflicts many people but is not so easily explained is the use of *good* and *well*. Let's begin by pointing out that the two words are different parts of speech. Now think back to the eight basic parts of speech in the English language, which are nouns, pronouns, verbs, adverbs, adjectives, prepositions, conjunctions, and interjections. *Good* is an adjective, a word that describes a noun. *Well* is an adverb, a word that describes a verb (an action).

Here are some examples of sentences in which *good* is used correctly:

> There was a lot of good food at the party.
>
> Eating with your fingers is not generally considered good etiquette.
>
> Janis got good news when she went to the doctor.

Now here are some examples of sentences in which *good* is used incorrectly:

> Max did good on the test.
>
> The minister spoke good last Sunday.
>
> I love to go to my friend Carmen's house because her mother cooks so good.

In the first set of three sentences, *good* is used correctly because in each instance it is an adjective, which describes a noun (*good food*, *good etiquette*, *good news*). In the second set of sentences, *good* is used incorrectly because in each instance it is functioning as an adverb, which describes an action (*did good*, *spoke good*, *cooks good*) — but *good* is *not* an adverb. Keep in mind, however, that *good* can be a noun, as in "the public good" or "She limited television for the good of her son."

Now let's turn to the word *well*, which exists in numerous forms. As a noun, Merriam-Webster defines *well* as "an issue of water from the earth," as in, "She drank the cool water from the well." That *well* can also be metaphorical, as in, "She sank into a well of despair." It's easy enough to use *well* correctly when you're writing about an actual well or a metaphorical one, but when you start using *well* in its other forms, things get far more complicated.

When *well* is used as an adverb, it means "to do in a good and satisfactory way" ("He plays bridge well" or "She speaks French well") or "to do in a thorough manner" ("The baker mixed the batter well" or "She washed her hands well after working in the garden").

*Well* can also be used as an adjective, meaning "in good health," as in, "Terry didn't feel well after eating Mexican food." A less common use of *well* as an adjective means "sensible, advisable," as in, "She would do well to follow the instructions more precisely." Finally, *well* can be an interjection, as in, "Well, I never heard such a lie!"

One way to get a handle on the *good/well* problem is to recognize that you will primarily use *good* as an adjective describing a noun (*good food*, *good wine*, *good health*) and you will primarily use *well* as an adverb that is connected to a verb (*play well*, *live well*, *do well*).

The reason many people get stuck in the *good/well* trap is because *good* occasionally *can* be used as an adverb in place of *well* in certain colloquial expressions like, "She felt good when she got an A on her physics exam" or "I sure got Sam good with that last snowball, didn't I?" This informal usage sounds entirely right to most people's ears, so you won't lose points with such sentences unless you are engaged in very formal writing. It must sound right, however. "Felt good" sounds different to the ear than "spoke good," "played good," and "ate good" do, so pay close attention in these instances.

You can also improve your writing by substituting crisper words for *good* and *well*, which are generally considered to be "filler" words, bland and vague. For example, "Lisa is a good violinist" tells you a lot less than "Lisa is a skilled [or inspired or expert] violinist." Similarly, a sentence like "General Tool Inc. provides well for its employees" might be upgraded to "General Tool Inc. provides generously [or satisfactorily] for its employees." Otherwise put, *good* and *well* might not help you achieve the level of precision that you are striving for in your writing.

### 8. *no one*

*Good/well* was a tough one. Let's refresh ourselves by clearing up a simpler mistake that is epidemic. The words *no one* mean "no person, not a single person." Consider these sentences in which *no one* is used correctly:

No one knows the secret to my lasagna recipe.

There was no one better informed about current events than my father.

No one escapes death.

For some reason, a great many people in the world think that *noone* is a word. There is no such word. A sentence that reads "Noone knows the secret of my lasagna recipe" can never be right. End of story.

### 9. *who, whom*

Fasten your seat belts, because the next three issues are difficult to unpack. We'll start with the one that is perhaps the least challenging of the three: *who/whom*. The culprit here is the word *whom*, which strikes fear in the hearts of so many who have never understood how to use it and feel inadequate because they believe that the correct usage of *whom* is critical to the mastery of the English language. In fact, *whom* is a dying word. You'll rarely hear it spoken or see it written, and you may never be called upon to use it, so by no means should you allow it to terrorize you.

Here is the difference between *who* and *whom*. *Who* is the subject form of the pronoun, as in these sentences:

Who killed Roger Rabbit?

Who was the thirty-second president of the United States?

*Whom* is the object form of the pronoun. Once again, the object is the thing that is acted upon in a sentence by the subject. The subject *does something* to the object, as in these sentences:

Distracted by the antics of her cat, Ellen momentarily forgot to whom she was speaking on the phone.

To whom should I address this letter?

One easy way to figure out *who/whom* usage is to try substituting *he/him* or *she/her* for *who/whom*. If *he* or *she* works, then *who* will work. If *him* or *her* works, then *whom* will work.

What especially complicates the *who/whom* issue, however, is the fact that *whom* is a dying word, as I stated above. So these days if we rewrote the sentence "Distracted by the antics of her cat, Ellen momentarily forgot to whom she was speaking on the phone" to read "Distracted by the antics of her cat, Ellen momentarily forgot who she was speaking to on the phone," few people would have a problem with that. In fact, to most readers' eyes and ears, that second version would be less stiff and stuffy and more pleasing than the first. That's the kind of usage that we alluded to when we discussed colloquial versions of *good* above.

When certain usages become part of the common parlance, it makes us rethink what is right and what is wrong. In fact, *whom* is in such danger of becoming extinct that virtually the only instance of its usage that is still prevalent is in the salutation "To whom it may concern."

If you are unclear about how to use *whom*, you can avoid the word simply by rewriting your sentence. For instance, if a sentence is confusing you, such as, "To whom did you give a present at Christmas?" you could rewrite it to read, "To which friends did you give a present at Christmas?" That would eliminate the issue of *whom*, thereby putting you on surer ground.

## 10. *I, me, myself*

Incorrect usage of *I, me,* and *myself* is another perilous trap that many writers fall into. It's a somewhat complicated matter, but a few moments of focused concentration could obviate a lifetime of confusion. Here are the fundamentals:

- *I* is always — and exclusively — used as a subject, specifically a subject pronoun. "I went to La Strada for dinner" shows the correct usage of *I* as the subject of that sentence. "Janis and I went to La Strada for dinner" is also correct, as *Janis* and *I* are the two subjects of that sentence, and when there are two subjects, you have what is known as a *compound subject*.

- *I* is never used as an object. If you were to say, "Fred called out to Max and I," that would be incorrect. "Fred called out to Max and me" is correct; *me* and *Max* are the objects. A quick and easy way to test whether you are using *I* correctly in such a sentence is to take out the other object (two objects make up a *compound object*, directly analogous to a compound subject) and see if *I* still works in the sentence. If you take *Max* out of the sentence "Fred called out to Max and I," you're left with "Fred called out to I." Your ear will tell you that something is very wrong with that sentence. "Fred called out to me," on the other hand, sounds entirely right — because it is.

- *Me* is an *object pronoun*, used in two instances: when an action (verb) is being done to or for a person or when a preposition is referring to a person. "Richard gave me a lift to the station" shows a correct usage of *me*, in which *me* is an indirect object that receives an action (the giving of a lift). "Jane went for a walk with me" also shows a correct usage of *me*, in which *me* is the object of the preposition *with*.

One usage that often trips people up is the expression "between you and _____," as in the sentence, "Between you and _____, Emily is a real liar." So many people make a mistake with this particular locution that, to our ears, "Between you and I" and "Between you and me" might both sound right. In fact, however, if you recognize that *between* is a preposition, you will understand that *me* is the correct object of that preposition and the sentence should read, "Between you and me, Emily is a real liar."

Let us emphasize as well that just as *I* never functions as an object, *me* never functions as a subject. "Me want a cookie" is an example of a sentence in which *me* is functioning as a subject, but unless you want to sound like the Cookie Monster, you should avoid that usage.

- *Myself* is a reflexive pronoun that is used when a writer is referring to him- or herself. Otherwise put, a writer will use the word *myself* when she both performs and receives the action of the verb: "I like myself best when I am organized and attentive to my responsibilities." The writer is performing the action (she is doing the liking) and receiving the action (she is the one being liked). Here are a few other examples of correct usage of *myself*:

I often cut myself shaving.

I'm going to hate myself in the morning.

I would describe myself as a generalist who is good at many things.

When the writer is *not* the subject of the sentence but *is* the object, then use *me*, because *me* always functions as an object in a sentence: "People describe me as a generalist." When the writer is *both* the subject and the object, use *myself*: "I describe myself as a generalist." A quick mnemonic tool for remembering this is that both *myself* and *subject* have an *s* in them.

## 11. *all right, alright; all ready, already; all together, altogether*

- *All right* means "everything is okay."
  *Alright* is not a word. Strike it from your list. Easy peasy.
- *All ready* means "completely ready" ("I was all ready to go to the movie, but then the phone rang").
  *Already* is an adverb that means "by this time" or "by the time mentioned" ("I was already in the house when I realized that I left the lights on in the car" or "Barack Obama is already recognized as one of our great presidents").
- *All together* means "as one" ("The ensemble played all together at the end" or "Jack, Ellen, and Frieda went to the party all together").
  *Altogether* is an adverb that can mean "completely" ("Hungarian is an altogether impenetrable language" or "I find it altogether impossible to argue

with you in a constructive way"). It can also mean "all things considered" or "given everything" ("Altogether, I would rather go to the dentist than to the opera" or "Altogether, dieting rarely works").

Altogether, using these terms correctly will clear up many common grammatical mistakes.

## 12. *that, which*

The difference between *that* and *which* is another source of confusion for many writers. To clear things up, let's begin by explaining the difference between an *essential clause* and a *nonessential clause*. (Or maybe we should back up even farther and remind ourselves that a *clause* is a group of words — not a sentence — that contains a subject and a verb.) An essential clause is designed to furnish information that is necessary to convey meaning; without that essential information, the sentence becomes meaningless. Consider a sentence like this, for instance: "I can remember the day that I met the person who went on to become my best friend." Without the clause "that I met the person who went on to become my best friend," the sentence reads, "I can remember the day," which obviously it makes no sense in this context because it doesn't provide the needed (essential) information to convey the thought.

Because little in English is genuinely easy, please note that it is acceptable to drop the word *that* in many uses of this sort. No one will take off points if you write, "I can remember the day I met the person who went on to become my best friend." There is no hard and fast rule about retaining or eliminating *that* in such sentences, however. It's more a matter of ear. Sometimes it sounds right to have it; sometimes it feels unnecessary.

Now, getting back to the core issues here, a *nonessential clause* is a clause that is not essential to a sentence, meaning that the sentence will make sense without it. For example, consider the sentence, "I met Emily, who has been my best friend all my life, at summer camp when I was twelve." If you take out the nonessential clause — "who has been my best friend all my life" — you are still left with a sentence that makes sense, "I met Emily at summer camp when I was twelve."

Typically, essential clauses are connected to main clauses with pronouns like *that*, *who*, or *where* ("I hate dogs that smell," "I would like to know who moved the cheese," "I wonder where I could find good Chinese food in this town").

Nonessential clauses are set off from the rest of the sentence by commas and are introduced with *which* when they refer to inanimate objects ("The diamond, which I inherited from my mother, was four karats," "Indian food, which I mostly avoid, tends to give me heartburn"). If a nonessential clause refers to a person, it begins with *who* and might look like this: "Claudia, who was my nanny growing up, lives comfortably in retirement in New Jersey." The word *which* never refers to a person.

Now, all of that said, many writers and even style guides regard the use of *which* in essential clauses as perfectly legitimate. That is certainly the case in British writing. You will not get into any significant trouble if you happen to use *which* in an essential clause — but *that* is preferable in such situations.

### 13. *insure, ensure*

Many writers frequently confuse *insure* and *ensure*. You insure something valuable: a Van Gogh painting, your grandmother's emerald brooch, your life. "People who live near the Mississippi River know how important it is to insure their houses against flood damage."

The word *ensure* means "to make certain," as in the sentence, "One way to ensure a sound future is through careful financial planning." The word *ensure* is often thought of as a rather stuffy word, smacking of legal jargon, so you might be better off using the phrase *make sure* instead of *ensure*, as in, "One way to make sure your future is sound is through careful financial planning."

### 14. *farther, further*

*Farther* refers to distance, as in, "The settlers traveled farther in search of arable land." The word *further* suggests "more of something." That something could be time, degree, or quality, as in, "Further investigation into the murder revealed conspiracy" or "The judge instructed the jury to return to the jury room for further deliberation."

### 15. *toward, towards*

*Toward* and *towards* mean exactly the same thing, but American usage prefers *toward* while British usage prefers *towards*. Quite a few writers use terms that hearken back to British antecedents when it would be preferable to use American spellings. For instance, I often see papers that have the word *travelled* in them. Brits still use the two-*l* approach when adding suffixes to words that end in *l*, like *travel* (*travelled*) or *fuel* (*fuelled*). Brits also like to keep the *e* in words like *sizeable*, *likeable*, and *liveable*, while Americans drop that *e*. Brits write *grey*, whereas American editors prefer *gray*. Not huge mistakes, by any standard, but do catch them when you can.

## 16. alternate, alternative

An *alternate* choice is one that substitutes for a first choice, as in, "When Joan saw all the traffic on her iPhone directions, she chose an alternate route." An *alternative* choice is a choice that you make from a number of viable options, as in "Unable to live on her own, Roberta had to make plans for the future based on a number of alternatives." The verb *alternate*, which means to switch from one to the other, as in, "She alternated between hot and cold, rarely finding a comfortable middle ground," does not enter into the *alternate*/*alternative* discussion.

## 17. fewer, less

Can you distinguish between *fewer* and *less?* If you're like most people in the world, the answer is no. The word *fewer* is used with regard to individual units, as in, "Each year, there are fewer attendees at the graduation ceremony" or "There are far fewer honeybees today than there were twenty years ago." Some fussy writers tend to use the expression "fewer in number," which is just an example of more words adding up to less, with no extra meaning. *Less* is used when referring to matters of mass or bulk, as in, "There is less cereal in the box than there was yesterday" or "There is less joy in the world today."

## 18. *principle, principal*

The word *principle* is a noun that refers to "a basic truth, law, or assumption," as in, "The United States was founded on the principle of liberty and justice for all" or "Newtonian principles are at the heart of physics."

The word *principal* has two meanings. As a noun, it means "head" or "chief," as in the *principal* of a school or the *principal* of a firm. As an adjective, it means "head" or "chief," as in "The principal reason the Great Depression occurred is because US stock market prices plummeted on Black Tuesday."

## 19. *comprise, compose*

I often see a sentence like, "The Marx Brothers are comprised of Groucho, Harpo, and Chico." That is an incorrect use of the word *comprise*, which is a verb that is synonymous with "contain," as in, "The US Code comprises the laws of the land" or "Yosemite National Park comprises over a million square miles of pristine landscape." It is important to note that when you use the word *comprise*, it has to follow the biggest piece of what you're talking about ("Yosemite") with subsets of that piece ("a million square miles"). In other words, it would be incorrect to write, "A million square miles of pristine landscape comprise Yosemite National Park."

The word *comprise* is often confused with the word

*compose*, which means "to make up." Here is a sentence that correctly uses *compose*: "The National League is composed of fifteen baseball teams." You can see that the phrase *composed of* means the same as "is made up of," so the sentence could also read, "The National League is made up of fifteen baseball teams." It would be correct, however, to write, "The National League comprises fifteen baseball teams," with the word *comprise* meaning "contain." Indeed, you could rewrite that sentence to read, "The National League contains fifteen baseball teams."

Just to confuse the issue, the verb *compose* also refers to writing music, but that sense of the word doesn't enter into this discussion.

## 20. *lie, lay*

I've saved the hardest for last. Full disclosure: even I, eminent author of *Seven Steps to Confident Writing*, often feel less than confident when faced with *lie/lay*. Let's try to sort this out, however. *To lay* means "to put" or "to place" and requires a direct object to give the word meaning. Here are some examples of sentences in which *lay* is used correctly:

I lay the wreath on the grave.

Do not lay your handbag on the floor.

The chickens lay their eggs in the straw.

*To lie* means "to recline, rest, or stay" or "to take a position of rest." (*Lie* also means "an untruth," but that meaning is rarely confused.) Here are some sentences that correctly represent the reclining meaning of *lie*:

Won't you lie down next to me?

Let's lie in the grass and feel the sun on our faces.

Please don't lie in the bed with your shoes on.

You *lay* a blanket on the grass, but you *lie* down on the blanket in the grass.

So far, so good? Hopefully so, but complications can well ensue when the tenses vary. To sort this out, it is best to use a chart:

| LIE | | |
| --- | --- | --- |
| Tense | First Person | Third Person |
| Present | I lie on the couch. | She lies on the couch. |
| Past | I lay on the couch. | She lay on the couch. |
| Present perfect | I have lain on the couch. | She has lain on the couch. |
| Present progressive | I am lying on the couch. | She is lying on the couch. |

| LAY | | |
| --- | --- | --- |
| Tense | First Person | Third Person |
| Present | I lay down the wreath. | She lays down the wreath. |
| Past | I laid down the wreath. | She laid down the wreath. |
| Past perfect | I have laid down the wreath. | She has laid down the wreath. |
| Present progressive | I am laying down the wreath. | She is laying down the wreath. |

With regard to this chart, you may be wondering about the word *lain*, shown in the present perfect form of *lie*. You will probably go through life without ever writing the word *lain* — or speaking it or even reading it. It is a word that has become quite obscure in the English language, but now, if you do happen to come across it, you'll know what it is.

This wraps up our section on the Top Twenty most common mistakes you can learn to avoid, but hold on. We're not done yet. We still have a few more areas of lapidary work to explore.

## Controlling Commas

I am not going to provide an entire lesson on commas in this book. It is easy enough for you to find useful lessons online from any number of excellent grammar sources, like Grammarly or Grammar Girl. Just google "correct usage of commas" and you'll be all set. Instead, I'm going to use this short space to discuss one specific comma usage, the serial comma, of which I am a staunch proponent. The serial comma, sometimes referred to as the Oxford comma, comes before the final conjunction in a list. For example:

Tamales, enchiladas, and tacos are typical Mexican foods.

Red, white, and blue are the American colors.

At my dance school, I learned the waltz, the fox-trot, and the mambo.

Please note that it would not be incorrect to write, "Tamales, enchiladas and tacos are typical Mexican foods," omitting that comma after *enchiladas*. The serial comma is not required; rather, I am recommending it, and I do so because I feel that it imparts better clarity to that kind of list.

Again, I refer you to the many online lessons that will help you get your comma usage under control, but let's move on to another problem area: the dreaded semicolon.

## Life without Semicolons

The great American writer Kurt Vonnegut was once quoted as warning writers away from semicolons, claiming that they would show only that the writer had been to college. I cannot say whether Vonnegut was serious when he said that, but I will say that I essentially agree with that assessment. The short and skinny on semicolons, as I routinely see them used, or misused, is that you can, and probably should, live without them. Most writers get very confused about them, and they crop up in the most unexpected and absurd places.

This is not to say that a semicolon is not a useful thing in the hands of a skilled writer who knows how to use it for the purpose of giving parts of a sentence that are closely related a more distinct break than one can get from a comma. In the hands of such writers, the semicolon helps to develop complex sentences that spool on in often thrilling ways. But ask yourself this: Are you such a writer (yet)? If not, and if you're drawn to the semicolon, as so many of my amateur writers are, then you're apt to fall into a trap that you have no idea how to get out of.

## Proofreading 101

As we come to the end of this step, let us spend a few moments reviewing the fine art of proofreading. Proofreading gives your work a final polish, as you check for and correct mistakes and make last-minute improvements. Proofreading plays a critical part in the writing process.

The key to productive proofreading is to be able to see your writing with fresh — or fresher — eyes. It's quite likely that you have gone over a piece of writing twenty times. If that's the case, you should be commended for your care and diligence, but you may still have tired eyes. Fortunately, some tricks of the trade can help you enliven those orbs. Try these methods:

- **Rest.** You may just need to step away from your writing for a few hours — or, better yet, if time permits, a few days. Things can look very different after such a hiatus.

- **Print.** Don't limit your proofreading to corrections you make while looking at your work on a computer screen. Print out your work and proofread from hard copy. It may not be the most ecological approach, but I bet you will find more errors that way. Printing out hard copy also allows you to try another trick of the trade, which involves taking a ruler or some other means of blocking out copy and looking at sentences one at a time.

- **Enlarge.** It may be even more ecologically incorrect, but if you blow your font size up a few notches, let's say from 11 to 16, your eyes are going to wake up and you will see things you haven't seen before. Trust me. You can even try changing the color of the type, if that helps. Printing in two columns is another way to see the text differently.

- **Specify.** Surprise those tired eyes by proofreading for one kind of mistake at a time. In other words, read your work over once for catching comma mistakes. Circle and examine every comma on the hard copy you've printed out. Do the same with quotation marks and whatever else makes sense.

When it comes to proofreading, it's all a matter of what works for you. Over time, you should develop a method that nets you the most catches. For instance, some people even read their work backward in the hunt for mistakes. Don't knock it till you've tried it.

## The End

Most pieces of writing reach an end point. They are either published, which means that changes cannot be made unless the work is reprinted or revised, or they are submitted (to a newspaper, a journal, a teacher, etc.), or they are stashed away.

Some works, however, are in progress for decades. There was a notable novel entitled *Miss MacIntosh, My Darling*, by Marguerite Young, which was begun in 1947 and published in 1965. Young worked on it every day for seventeen years and submitted a manuscript to her publisher that was 3,449 pages. When it was published, as a novel of 1,198 pages, it was received with enthusiasm. The *New York Times Book Review* called it "a work of stunning magnitude and beauty ...a masterwork." Young confessed that, had she known it would take that long to write the novel, she would never have taken it on. Kudos to Ms. Young, but that piece of writing, as many years as it took to complete it, also reached its end point.

Writing requires enormous effort, but there is also enormous satisfaction in bringing a piece of writing to its best state. As I said earlier, there is nothing I like more than watching my student writers experience the exhilaration that comes with burnishing their writing to a fine glow. There is nothing that makes me prouder than to know that I have inspired a sense of ownership in my students toward their writing, so that they commit to it, work at it, and for the most part succeed with it.

You can do the same. You can become a confident writer who feels that same sense of ownership and exhilaration. To that end, I advise you to work at your writing with the understanding that learning about writing never ends. I'm still learning — whenever, wherever, however I can.

## Up Close

Before there were computers, writers worked by hand on manuscript pages that, at times, resembled the incredibly intricate cuneiform of ancient cultures. Today, with computer-generated manuscripts, it is not so easy to capture the visuals of editing. So for this last chapter I thought it would be interesting for you to see what lapidary work looked like for two eminent writers:

Edith Wharton's *The House of Mirth* (1905)
*From Edith Wharton Collection, Yale Collection of American Literature,*
*Beinecke Rare Book and Manuscript Library*

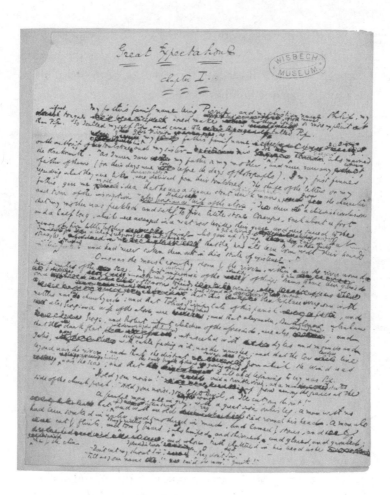

Charles Dickens's *Great Expectations* (1861)
*Courtesy of the Wisbech and Fenland Museum*
*(www.wisbechmuseum.org.uk)*

What is the takeaway from these two examples? That writing is, as I said, ve~~ry hard~~ work. Consider the payoff, however. We are still reading these works, both of which go back more than one hundred years.

This is a good time too to collect some of the best writing tips from some of the best writers. Consider the following:

If it sounds like writing, I rewrite it.
> — Elmore Leonard, author of *Get Shorty*
> and *Jackie Brown*

Never use a metaphor, simile, or other figure of speech which you are used to seeing in print.
> — George Orwell, author of *1984* and *Animal Farm*

Kill your darlings, kill your darlings, even when it breaks your egocentric little scribbler's heart, kill your darlings.
> — Stephen King, author of *Misery* and *The Shining*

Substitute "damn" every time you're inclined to write "very"; your editor will delete it and the writing will be just as it should be.
> — Mark Twain, author of *The Adventures of*
> *Huckleberry Finn* and *Life on the Mississippi*

If you are using dialogue — say it aloud as you write it. Only then will it have the sound of speech.
> — John Steinbeck, author of *The Grapes of Wrath*
> and *Of Mice and Men*

> Cut out all those exclamation marks. An exclamation mark is like laughing at your own joke.

>> — F. Scott Fitzgerald, author of
>> *The Great Gatsby* and *Tender Is the Night*

> You can't wait for inspiration. You have to go after it with a club.

>> — Jack London, author of
>> *The Call of the Wild* and *White Fang*

Prose is architecture, not interior decoration.

> — Ernest Hemingway, author of
> *A Farewell to Arms* and *The Old Man and the Sea*

If a sentence, no matter how excellent, does not illuminate your subject in some new and useful way, scratch it out.

> — Kurt Vonnegut, author of
> *Slaughterhouse Five* and *Cat's Cradle*

> Read, read, read. Read everything — trash, classics, good and bad, and see how they do it. Just like a carpenter who works as an apprentice and studies the master. Read! You'll absorb it. Then write. If it's good, you'll find out. If it's not, throw it out of the window.

>> — William Faulkner, author of
>> *The Sound and the Fury* and *Light in August*

## ROUNDUP

1. Prune, prune, prune. Never waste your reader's time and attention.
2. Adverbs and adjectives are good candidates for pruning.
3. Qualifiers like *really*, *very*, and *just* should always be questioned.
4. Avoid unnecessary pairing of words, like "each and every" or "fair and pleasant," which add up to more words.
5. A good point doesn't become better simply because you repeat it.
6. Don't dither with expressions like "it seems" or "I think." Just say what you want to say.
7. Steer clear of nominalizations, which turn verbs into noun phrases.
8. Vague pronouns will bring down the level of your writing. Make a point of catching them.
9. Work at catching the Top Twenty "don'ts" that account for the most typical writing mistakes.
10. Discover and use the serial comma.
11. Avoid semicolons unless you are absolutely clear on how to use them.
12. The four-point method of effective proofreading is based on Rest, Print, Enlarge, and Specify.

# Acknowledgments

Thank you to my agent, Reiko Davis, of DeFiore and Company, for her interest in my writing and for helping me spread the cause of good writing to others.

Thanks to Jason Gardner, my editor, who has been most responsive and supportive of this book.

I would also like to thank the copy editor, Ann Moru. Copy editors are too often unsung, but in fact they play a crucial role in a book's publication. Also, I like to tell my students that when I get something back from a copy editor, it often has just as many red marks as when they get something back from me.

We can all use help with our writing. And help in our lives at large — so a very big thank-you to my wife, Karen Levine, for all her support through my many long and often difficult years as a writer.

# Index

acronyms, internet, 182, 197
ACT exam, 184
Adams, Douglas, 33
adjectives, 126–27; adverbs confused as, 215–18; grammatical purpose of, 101; minimized use of, 11, 108, 201–2; possessive, 208; pruning of, 240
adverbs, 126–27, 223–24; adjectives confused as, 215–18; avoidance of, in attributions, 189; conjunctive, 210–11; flabby writing and overuse of, 184–85; grammatical purpose of, 102; minimized use of, 11, 108, 201–2; pruning of, 240
*affect/effect* confusions, 213–14

Alcott, Louisa May, 176
*all ready / already* usage, 223
*all right*, correct usage of, 223
*all together / altogether* usage, 223–24
*a lot / allot / alot* confusions, 214–15
*alternate / alternative* usage, 227
*Amazing Adventures of Kavalier & Clay, The* (Chabon), 176
*Ambassadors, The* (James), 108–9
ambiguity, 10–11
*American Scholar, The* (magazine), 96
analyzing, 48
*Anna Karenina* (Tolstoy), 146–47
antecedents, 206–7

applying, 48–49
arch expressions, 12
arguing, 49
articles, 100
Asbury, Herbert, 56
*As I Lay Dying* (Faulkner), 175
associating, 48
*Atlantic* (magazine), 23
attributions, 189, 197
Atwood, Margaret, 175
audience: communication style
    and, 2–5; identifying, 1–2, 5–9,
    29, 42, 61; tone and, 165–66;
    Up Close exercise, 24–29; writ-
    er's contract with, 9–13, 28–29;
    writing to, xi. *See also* reader
Austen, Jane, 146–47
authentic voice, 162–67
autism, 4

backstory, 136
bathos, 104–5
Baumbach, Noah, 34
*Being Mortal* (Gawande), 58
Bible, 75
*Blind Assassin, The* (Atwood), 175
Bookfox (writing blog), 94
Book-of-the-Month Club, 130
book reviews, 23
brainstorming, 38, 46–50, 51, 61
British usages, 225, 226–27
Bulwer-Lytton, Edward, 16
business jargon, 179
buzzwords, 182

capitalization, 100
*Catcher in the Rye, The* (Salinger),
    10
causality, 116
Chabon, Michael, 176
chapters, 145
*Charlotte's Web* (White), 95
clarity, xi, 10–11, 14, 29
clauses: conjunctions connecting,
    102; defined, 224; dependent
    (subordinate), 114, 115–17,
    118–19, 121–22; essential vs.
    nonessential, 224–25; indepen-
    dent, 114–17, 121–22; types of,
    123
cleverness, 138, 139, 151–52, 153
clichés, 16, 17, 135, 143, 170–71,
    176, 197
clustering, 49–50
Coe, Jonathan, 94
college-admission essays: concept
    in, 134–35; dialogue in, 188–89;
    objective of, 65; problematic
    writing in, 104–6; storytelling
    in, 66–68, 76–77, 82–84; tone
    issues in, 190–96; Up Close
    exercises involving, 24–29,
    190–96; word limits of, 201
colloquial language, 170, 196,
    217–18
color, 12, 14, 29, 156
*Color Purple, The* (Walker), 75
commas, 118–19, 231–32, 234, 240;
    Oxford, 231–32, 240

comma splices, 122, 127
commitment, 13, 14–15, 28–29, 182
Common Core standards, 98
communication style, 2–5, 29, 192
comparing, 47–48
competence, 182
*comprise/compose* usage, 228–29
computers, 233–34, 235
concept: first draft issues of,
    134–35, 159; second draft issues
    of, 138–39; third draft issues of,
    142; Up Close exercises involv-
    ing, 151–52, 153
conciseness, xi; literary examples
    of, 162; pruning for, 73–74,
    200–205; qualifiers omitted for,
    171; in writer-reader contract,
    11, 14, 29
conclusions. *See* endings
confidence: authentic voice and,
    164–66; lack of, 109–10, 172, 173
conflict, 78–81, 84, 86, 138–40,
    142, 152–53
conjunctions, 126–27, 211–12; co-
    ordinating, 102, 115–16, 117–18;
    defined, 210; subordinating,
    117, 118–19, 121–22
conjunctive adverbs, 210–11
construction, 11, 29
content, 139–40, 142, 169
contractions, 170, 196, 209
copywriting, 130–31, 165–66
Cormier, Robert, 34
courtesy, 12, 29

creative brief, 41
creative writing, 98
crossword puzzles, 187
cubing, 47–49
cutting and pasting, 141

*Daily Beast*, 55–58
dazzle, 134
deadlines, 37, 42, 61
Defoe, Daniel, 80
describing, 47
*Devil in the White City, The*
    (Larson), 10
diagramming, 97–98
dialogue, 156, 187–90, 197, 238
Dickens, Charles, 237
dictionaries, 186–87, 197
Dillard, Annie, 93, 99
direct objects, 111–13
discernment, 22
discipline, 13–15, 19–22
distractions, 34–35
dithering, 203, 240
drafts: commitment and, 13,
    14–15, 28–29; first, 133–37, 140,
    141–42, 159; flow of, 131–32,
    141; focus/purpose of, 15,
    132–33, 159; lack of under-
    standing about, 18; of openings,
    148; polishing/proofreading,
    143–44, 160; second, 138–41,
    160; third, 141–43, 160; Up
    Close exercise, 151–59; writing
    process and, 131–32

Draper, Don, 80
Dr. Seuss, 183
Duke, Marshall, 56

editing process, 199–200
*Elements of Style, The* (Strunk and
    White), 95
Elley, W. B., 98
Ellington, Duke, 113
emails: courtesy in, 12; fear level
    and, 33; writing a project as,
    46, 61
emotion, 152–53, 156
empowerment, 182
endings, 60, 137, 147, 148–51, 160
*ensure*, correct usage of, 226
entertainment jargon, 178–79
essays: drafting of, 132; legacy,
    54–58. *See also* college-
    admission essays
examples, 59–60
exclamation marks, 239
"Experimental Study of Apparent
    Behavior, An" (Heider and
    Simmel), 64
exposition, 189, 197
Extraordinary, The, 77–78, 83–84,
    86

"fades," 149
FAQ, 182
*Farewell to Arms, A* (Hemingway),
    143
*farther*, correct usage of, 226
Faulkner, William, 32, 94, 175, 239

fear, 31, 32–34, 60
Feldenkrais, Moshé, xiii
Feldenkrais Method, xiii, 15
*fewer*, correct usage of, 227–28
*Fight Club* (film; 1999), 80
"filler" words, 218
Fitzgerald, F. Scott, 239
Flaubert, Gustave, 184
font size, 233–34, 240
formality, 167–74, 185–86, 196–97,
    217–18
Fox, Laurie, 130
frames, 78–81
freewriting, 43–45, 61
fundraising letters, 182
*further*, correct usage of, 226
fustiness, 110, 172
FWIW, 182

*Gangs of New York, The* (Asbury),
    56
Gawande, Atul, 58
gender stereotypes, 157
gerunds, 122
goals, 182
Goethe, Johann Wolfgang von, 33
*Golfweek*, 74
*good/well* problem, 215–18
Google, 17, 35, 148
grammar checkers, 171, 207
Grammar Girl, 231
grammar instruction, 98
grammar lapses, 144
Grammarly, 231
*Great Expectations* (Dickens), 237

*Having the Last Say* (Gelb), xi,
54–55
Heider, Fritz, 64
Hemingway, Ernest, 107–8,
111–12, 123, 143, 162, 239
*His Dark Materials* (Pullman), 63
homophobia, 157
*House of Mirth, The* (Wharton),
236

*I*, correct usage of, 220, 222
IMHO, 182
imperatives, 170, 196
inaccessible communicator, 3, 29,
109
inappropriate communicator, 3, 29
inconsiderate communicator, 3, 29
indirect objects, 111, 112–13
inexact communicator, 3, 29
informality, 167–74, 217–18
*in media res* openings, 83, 147, 159
insecure communicator, 3, 29
inspiration, 239
*insure*, correct usage of, 226
interjections, 103, 126–27, 170
internet, 34–35, 42, 148, 182, 197,
231
"invisible cuts," 74, 201–4
*it's / its* confusions, 209–10

James, Henry, 94, 108–9, 119, 162
jargon, 135, 143, 166, 177–80, 197.
*See also* legalisms
job applications, 33, 123–26
journaling, 42, 50–51, 61

Joyce, James, 32, 94, 201
judgment, suspending, 22–24,
29, 47

Kafka, Franz, 80
Kellogg, Brainerd, 98
Kerouac, Jack, 35
King, Stephen, 238

language: amping up, 156; colloquial, 170, 196, 217–18; "of
the day," 166; legal, 9, 151, 153,
180–81, 182; spoken, 120
lapidary work: defined, 199;
during editing process,
199–200; of famous authors,
235–37; pronoun vagueness,
205–7, 240; proofreading,
233–34, 240; pruning, 200–205,
240; punctuation, 231–32, 240;
technical errors, 207–31, 240;
Up Close exercise, 235–39. *See
also* technical errors
Larson, Erik, 10
*lay*, correct usage of, 229–31
*Leaves of Grass* (Whitman), 23
legalisms, 9, 151, 153, 180–81, 182,
226
Leonard, Elmore, 190, 238
*less*, correct usage of, 227–28
Letterman, David, 151–52
letters: of complaint, xiii, 1–2, 140,
142–43, 144; cover, 123–26,
124n, 144; drafting of, 132; to
the editor, xiv, 1, 86–90;

letters (*continued*)
  fundraising, 182; personal, 1;
  tone considerations in, 167–71;
  writing a project as, 46, 61
*lie*, correct usage of, 229–31
life reviews, xi–xii, 54–58
"Lifesaving Power of Storytelling,
  The" (Gelb), 55–58
linear structure, 159
listening, 166, 190
literature, 98, 175–76, 235–39
*Little Women* (Alcott), 176
LOL, 182
*Lolita* (Nabokov), 23, 146–47
London, Jack, 50, 239
*lose / loose* confusions, 212–13

*Madame Bovary* (Flaubert), 184
*Mad Men* (TV series), 80
Mamet, David, 190
mapping, 49–50
McCullers, Carson, 32
*me*, correct usage of, 221–23
Melville, Herman, 75
metaphors, 11, 135, 143, 174–76,
  197, 238
midsection, 137
*Miss MacIntosh, My Darling*
  (Young), 234–35
*Moby Dick* (Melville), 75
Morrison, Toni, 96–97, 99
motivators, intrinsic, 36–37
*myself*, correct usage of, 222–23

Nabokov, Vladimir, 23, 146–47
narrative, 78, 79. *See also* storytelling
narrative flair, 67–68
negativity, 204
*New American Review*, 129
*New York Times*, 23
*New York Times Book Review*, 235
nominalizations, 204, 240
nonprofit world buzzwords, 182
*no one*, 218
notebooks, 50–51
noun phrases, 204, 240
nouns, 100, 108, 111, 126–27

objects, 111–13, 221–22
Once, The, 74–77, 79, 83, 86
openings, 83, 134, 136–37, 146–48,
  150–51, 160
opportunity, 182
Ordinary vs. Extraordinary,
  77–78, 83–84, 86
Orwell, George, 13–14, 238
outlining, 52–54, 61
Oxford comma, 231–32, 240

pairs, avoiding, 202–3, 240
Palahniuk, Chuck, 80
paragraphs, 145–46, 160
Parker, Dorothy, 32
participles, dangling, 122
parts of speech, 100–103, 123, 215.
  *See also specific part of speech*

passion, 182

passive voice, 172–74, 197, 203

performance anxiety, 17

phrases, 102, 113

"Pit and the Pendulum, The" (Poe), 10

*Plain English for Lawyers* (Wydick), 180

Poe, Edgar Allan, 10, 32

Point, The, 81–82, 84, 86, 142–43, 150, 160

point of view, 200

polishing, 143–44, 159, 160

positivity, 204

possessive adjectives, 208

possessive pronouns, 208, 210

potential, 182

predicates, 103–11, 112, 123, 127

prepositional phrases, 113

prepositions, 102, 126–27

presentation, 135–36, 142, 159

*Pride and Prejudice* (Austen), 146–47

*principle/principal* usage, 227–28

printing out, 233, 240

procrastination, 33, 34–38, 59, 60–61, 132, 133

pronouns, 126–27; essential clauses and, 225; grammatical purpose of, 100–101; object, 111, 221–22; possessive, 208, 210; reflexive, 222–23; vague, 205–7, 240

proofreading, 144, 160, 233–34, 240

proportion, 137

pruning, 200–205, 239, 240

Pullman, Philip, 63

punctuation, 11, 118, 240. *See also* commas; comma splices; semicolons

Pynchon, Thomas, 201

qualifiers, 149–50, 171, 196, 202, 238, 240

questions: for audience identification, 8–9, 29; at beginning of writing process, 38–41, 59–60, 61; writers and, 38; about writing history, 16–19

quotas, 35–36, 37, 42, 61

quotations, 148

racial stereotypes, 157

reader: alienating, 12; communicating with, 2–5; The Point and, 82; visualizing, 1–2, 5–9, 29, 42, 61; writer's contract with, xi, 9–13, 29, 73–74, 200–201. *See also* audience

reading, 186–87, 190, 197, 239

Reed, Alonzo, 98

relearning, 15–19, 29

repetition, 203, 240

research, 42–43, 61

restaurant reviews, 47–49, 53–54

resting, before proofreading, 233, 240

reviews: life, xi–xii, 54–58; literary, 23; restaurant, 47–49, 53–54

rewriting process, 129–30, 141, 238. *See also* drafts

rhythm, 6, 24, 123, 145–46, 190

rigidity, 15

rigor, 14–15, 28–29

"Role of Grammar in a Secondary School Curriculum, The" (Elley et al.), 98

*Romeo and Juliet* (Shakespeare), 80

*Rotters' Club, The* (Coe), 94

Rudnick, Paul, 34

rules, 44, 45, 46, 94, 98, 106–7, 171–72

Saddleback College, 124n

Salinger, J. D., 10

Santayana, George, 148

sarcasm, 12

SAT exam, 184

scaffold, 52–54, 61

Scrabble (word game), 187

self-editing, 18, 40

semicolons, 118, 121, 232, 240

sentences: appreciating, 93–97, 99, 126, 183; comma splices, 122, 127; complex, 114, 118–19, 126, 127; compound, 114, 117–18, 121, 126, 127; compound-complex, 114, 119–20, 126, 127; experimenting with, 111; fragments, 114, 120, 127; long, 94–95; parts of speech, 100–103, 123, 126–27, 215; pruning, 239; rhythm of, 123; run-on, 96, 114, 121–22, 127; short, 108; simple, 114, 117, 126, 127; structuring, xi, 97–99; subjects/predicates in, 103–11, 127; Up Close exercise, 123–26; variations in, 113–20, 122–23, 125–26, 127

serial comma, 231–32, 240

sexual stereotypes, 157

Shakespeare, William, 80

Shelley, Percy Bysshe, 35

similes, 174–76, 197, 238

Simmel, Marianne, 64

six Cs, 10–13

slang, 135, 161

snarkiness, 12

Solotoroff, Ted, 129–30

Sorkin, Aaron, 190

specificity, during proofreading, 234, 240

speech, parts of, 100–103, 123, 215. *See also specific part of speech*

speeches, 132

spell checkers, 171, 207

spelling, 19

sports jargon, 179

Steinbeck, John, 238

stereotypes, 157

storytelling, 24; in college-admission essays, 65, 66–68; critical elements of, 71, 74–82,

83–84, 86, 138; human tradition of, 63–65; learnability of, 68; as natural, 68; power of, 55–58, 82–86; resistance to, 65–66; sample drafts, 69–74; Up Close exercise, 86–91

structure: audience and, 6; decision making about, 59; during editing process, 200; first draft issues of, 136–37, 140, 159; linear, 159; paragraphs and, 145–46, 160; The Point supported by, 140; polishing and, 143–44; second draft issues of, 140, 160; third draft issues of, 142

Strunk, William, Jr., 95

*Stuart Little* (White), 95–96

subjects, 103–11, 112, 120, 123, 127, 221

*Sula* (Morrison), 96–97

*Sun Also Rises, The* (Hemingway), 107–8, 111–12, 123

*Superman* (comic), 80

symbolic imagery, 162

syntax, 100

tags, 149

TBH, 182

technical errors, 240; *affect/effect*, 213–14; *all ready / already*, 223; *all right / alright*, 223; *all together / altogether*, 223–24; *a lot / allot / alot*, 214–15; *alternate / alternative*, 227; *comprise/*

*compose*, 228–29; *farther/further*, 226; *fewer/less*, 227–28; *good/well*, 215–18; *I/me/myself*, 220–23; *insure/ensure*, 226; *it's/its*, 209–10; *lie/lay*, 229–31; *lose/loose*, 212–13; *no one*, 218; *principle/principal*, 227–28; *that/which*, 224–25; *their/there*, 207–9; *then/than*, 210–12; *toward/towards*, 226–27; *who/whom*, 219–20

technology, 141

tense, 26, 101, 132, 200

tension, 78–81, 84, 86, 96–97

texting, 182

*that/which* usage, 224–25

*their/there* confusions, 207–9

*then/than* confusions, 210–12

thought, completion of, 120

time, 74–75, 79, 101, 132

toasts, xiii–xiv, 84–86, 138–39, 151–59

Tolstoy, Leo, 146–47

tone: audience and, 6; clichés/jargon and, 176–81, 197; dialogue and, 187–90, 197; during editing process, 200; finding authentic voice for, 162–67, 181, 196; first draft issues of, 135; formal vs. informal, 167–74, 196–97, 217–18; metaphors/similes and, 174–76, 197; negative vs. positive, 204; The Point supported by, 140; polishing, 159; sensitivity to, xi; third draft

tone (*continued*)
  issues of, 143; transgressions of, 161–62, 182–83, 197; Up Close exercises, 190–96; vocabulary and, 183–87, 197
*To the Lighthouse* (Woolf), 175
*toward/towards* usage, 226–27
transformation, 182
*Trial, The* (Kafka), 80
trial and error, 75
Twain, Mark, 238

*Ulysses* (Joyce), 94
"unsaid," the, 162
Up Close exercises: about, 24; audience identification, 24–29; drafts, 151–59; lapidary work, 235–39; sentences, 123–26; storytelling, 86–91; tone, 190–96; writing process, 54–60
usage, 219–20

verbs, 101, 108, 204, 240
vocabulary, xi, 108, 110, 183–87, 197
voice: authentic, 162–67, 181, 196; passive vs. active, 172–74, 197, 203; quality of, 143
Vonnegut, Kurt, 232, 239

Walker, Alice, 75
webbing, 49–50
*well/good* problem, 215–18
Wharton, Edith, 236

*which/that* usage, 224–25
White, E. B., 95–96
Whitman, Walt, 23
*who/whom* usage, 219–20
willpower, 19
Windsor, Duchess of, 130
Woolf, Virginia, 175
word acquisition, 183–87, 197
word choice, 143, 157, 170, 184–85, 194, 218
word games, 187, 197
word-processing tools, 207
writer: contract with himself/herself, 13–15, 29; contract with reader, xi, 9–13, 29, 73–74, 200–201; questions and, 38
writing: as aural experience, 113, 137, 150–51, 188, 197; clumsy, 109–11; as communication, 29, 31; copywriting, 130–31, 165–66; creative, 98; "death of," ix; discipline of, 19–22, 29; end point of, 234–35; exercises for beginning, 20–22, 29; fear of, 31, 32–34; flabby, 184–85; flexibility in, 141; fluency in, 51; importance of, xiii–xiv; improvements in, ix–xii, 23–24; joy of, 44; as natural, xii, 15–16; natural gift for, 17, 99; persuasive, 12; relearning, xii–xiii, 15–19, 29; rich, 119; suspended judgment for, 22–24, 29, 47; teaching of, 44; texting vs., 182;

tips for, 238–39; writer/reader contract underlying, 31. *See also* writing process

*Writing Life, The* (Dillard), 93

writing process, 159; brainstorming, 46–50, 61; freewriting, 43–45, 61; getting started, 38–42; getting unstuck, 42–43, 59–60; journaling, 50–51, 61; outline/scaffold, 52–54, 61; possible length of, 234–35; psychological impediments hindering, 31–38, 42, 58–59, 60–61, 132; understanding, xi, 131–33, 145; Up Close exercise, 54–60. *See also* drafts

writing schedules, 35

Wydick, Richard, 180

Young, Marguerite, 234–35

# About the Author

Alan Gelb has pursued a professional writing career for over forty years, publishing novels, works of nonfiction, young adult fiction, a play, and articles for publications like the *New York Times* and the *Daily Beast*. In recent years, he has published two books about writing: *Conquering the College Admissions Essay in 10 Steps* (3rd edition, Ten Speed Press, 2017) and *Having the Last Say: Capturing Your Legacy in One Small Story* (Tarcher Penguin, 2015). As a college essay coach, he works with students all over the world. You may visit Alan at www.conquerthecollegeessay.com and at www.alangelbwriter.com.